Please take note that advice and observations within this book are based on the choices I made for my children and that worked for us in our particular situation. It is not meant to take the place of, or override, the advice given by a doctor or mental health professional who has firsthand knowledge and understanding of your child and of your particular and unique situation. The intention of this book is to offer information and share the experiences I have had through my children in hopes of supporting others as they the search for spiritual understanding, growth, and well-being.

A Knowing
Living with Psychic Children

authorHOUSE

AuthorHouse™
1663 Liberty Drive, Suite 200
Bloomington, IN 47403
www.authorhouse.com
Phone: 1-800-839-8640

© 2010 Christina A. Pierson. All rights reserved.

No part of this book may be reproduced, stored in a retrieval system, or transmitted by any means without the written permission of the author.

First published by AuthorHouse 2/2/2010

ISBN: 978-1-4490-4940-9 (e)
ISBN: 978-1-4490-4938-6 (sc)
ISBN: 978-1-4490-4939-3 (hc)

Library of Congress Control Number: 2010900292

Printed in the United States of America
Bloomington, Indiana

This book is printed on acid-free paper.

Praise for

A Knowing – Living with Psychic Children

"This fascinating and very informative book is a must-have for any parent or carer who is struggling to understand, help and support their psychic child; in fact it is an important handbook to help anyone cope in such circumstances. Living with a psychic child can be both intriguing and frightening – in equal measure – and with Christina's help and vast personal experience her book will prove to be both an essential tool and an absorbing read. I highly recommend it."

-Jacqueline Harvey, Researcher

"This book is the most comprehensive presentation of psychic phenomena in children that I am aware of. Unlike anything that has come before it, this book illustrates through the words and drawings of children what the reality of a psychic child's experience is in truth. The ability to touch the child within is an extraordinary gift. Christina has it in abundance."

-John Collins, Irish Psychic and Intuitive Healer

About The Author

Christina Pierson DCH, ADCHP is a mother-of-three, a hypnotherapist, psychotherapist, Reiki Master, author, and speaker. She currently splits her time between the United States and Ireland as she continues to research psychic phenomena in children, as well as spiritual and metaphysical insights and healing through hypnosis. Christina can be reached through her website www.aknowing.com or her Facebook page *A Knowing – Living with Psychic Children (www.facebook.com/pages/A-Knowing-Living-With-Psychic-Children/).*

Do not believe in what you have heard

Do not believe in traditions because they have been handed down for many generations

Do not believe anything because it is rumored and spoken of by many

Do not believe merely because the written statements of some old sage are produced

Do not believe in conjectures

Do not believe in that as a truth to which you have become attached by habit

Do not believe merely on the authority of your teachers and elders

After observation and analysis, when it agrees with
reason and is conductive to the good
and benefit of one and all, then accept it and live up to it.

- Gautama Buddha

¤   ¤   ¤

There are more things in heaven and earth, Horatio,
Than are dreamt of in your philosophy

-Shakespeare, Hamlet Act 1 Scene 5

Contents

Chapter 1: Introduction 1

- The Beginning 1
- Yin & Yang 4
- Love, Understanding & No Fear 5
- Keep a Record 12
- The Psychic Connection 14
- A Knowing 17
- Love is All 20
- What's In This Book 21

Chapter 2: Jesus & the Angelic 22

- In Jesus' Tummy 23
- Missing Jesus 25
- Jesus' Picture 27
- Jesus' Visit 30
- Clouds & Multi-Colored Rain 39
- Blue Light 42
- Pink & Blue Light 43
- Voices Calling & Singing 46
- Angel of the Six Hearts 46
- Jesus: The Angel You Are 48

Chapter 3: Alien Encounters 51

- "Jesus" & the Flying Machine: Out-of-Body Experience 55
- The Reptilian & the Telescope: Dream Experience 58
- Red & Grey Aliens: Physical Experience 59

Chapter 4: Mystical Communications & Dreams   67

- God's Secret   69
- The Church Prayer   74
- The Garden   76
- Good & Evil   78
- It Looks Like God   80
- Khou-Sa-Heh-Yah   80
- The Grid   84
- Grey Lady in the Doorway   86
- A Friend   87
- Seeing Auras   91
- Guardian Angel   92
- The Inverted Pyramid   93

Chapter 5: The Dark Side   96

- Not Of This World   99
- Of This Earth   101
- The Black Doorway   103
- Bad Smells   105
- Doesn't Belong Here   108
- Choose Between Light & Dark   109
- The Man Who Destroyed God   111
- The Attack   114
- "Ghoul" in the Black Cloak   118
- Emotional & Energy Leeches   119
- Bellowing   122
- Ask, Listen and Raise Them Up   123
- Similar Visions: Years Apart   128
- Another Energy-Collector   130
- Dead Men Walking   132
- Figure Walking Through House   134

Chapter 6: Greater Insights — 137

- My Other Mother — 137
- When You Die You Still Live — 139
- More Than One Chance — 140
- All Happening Now — 142
- Angel, Devil, Vortex — 143
- Seeing With Your Mind — 145
- God's Name: No Right Way of Saying His Name — 145
- Anithe's Observations — 146
- "No" to Confirmation — 149
- Mediation & A Personal "Religion" — 152
- Our Reality, Our Experience — 156

Chapter 7: Helpful Hints — 161

- A Bit of Advice — 162
- Love, Intent, Belief, but No Fear — 165
- Psychic Shield — 166
- Pyramid of Light — 169
- Visualizations — 170
- House Clearing — 171
- Smudge Sticks & Incense — 172
- Sound — 173
- Salt Baths — 173
- Crystals — 174
- Meditation & Prayer — 175
- Authors — 175
- A Final "Sign" — 176
- Expect the Unexpected — 176
- Where's the Beef? — 178
- Speech given to UCC Psychological Society & World Ghost Convention 2007 — 182

Introduction

A Knowing – Living with Psychic Children is an unusual book in many ways, not the least of which is the volume and variety of the experiences that are contained within it. It is also unique in that it is the only work, that I am aware of, that extensively documents the psychic experiences of the same children over a ten year period. Having an open channel with my children has allowed them to share their many experiences with me that ranged from angelic interactions and benevolent alien encounters to the presence of dark entities. It is the result of years of collection, discussion, edification, and research.

This book is based purely on the experiences of my children, whose names I have changed within the text. As their type of experiences varied, some chapters are significantly shorter than others. All the pictures are ones that my children drew and that I collected over the years, so the quality is not always the best. Throughout this adventure with my kids, I never thought for a moment of writing a book about it, so the pictures came when they did, in the manner that they did, and so be it. My apologies, however, for the lack of clarity and any fingerprints that may be visible! These drawings are important because they illustrate what the children were experiencing much better than anything I can describe. It is vital for parents and those who care for children to realize that often the simplest and most seemingly insignificant art can represent something very powerful and revealing. We must develop the skill of being able to identify and discover large truths within very small details as well as discover the deep meaning hidden within the limited vocabulary of children. So take note of children's drawings, ask questions, but don't project. Remember, sometimes a house is only a house and sometimes it represents the body that houses the soul. Only the children will know and they will explain.

Unfortunately, because of restrictions in printing this book, none of the pictures are in color. For the most part this has made little to no difference because my children drew in pencil or in a single color and that color was not of significance. But for a few of the drawings color is important in terms of effectively communicating what was experienced. In order to have the drawings available to you I have set up a website where you can view them all as they were meant to be seen and drawn by the children. The website is www.aknowing.com . You can also view them on my **Facebook Page,** *A Knowing - Living with Psychic Children (www.facebook. com/pages/ A-Knowing-Living-With-Psychic-Children/).* You can contact me directly through either venue with questions or comments.

    I hope people enjoy this book and find it informative, and also hope that those parents whose children have expressed psychic experiences and who may be fearful and feeling isolated will take heart, while I pray that all others who have not had first-hand experience will take note. These children have come to help us and to get our attention in the hopes of waking us up, but it is up to us to acknowledge and respond with acceptance and support.

Acknowledgements

First and foremost I would like to thank my children for their patience, their teachings, and their love. Without them this book would never have come into being and, more importantly, the knowledge and understanding of all the miracles and the activity that exists all around us would have gone unrecognized and unnoticed by me. You three have brought enlightenment, light, and love into my life and I am forever grateful for having been given the opportunity and the honor of being your mother.

I especially want to thank my parents, Andrée and Lee; my brother, Glen; and his partner, Charlie, for all their love and support and editing suggestions. Family is a foundation from which I have learned many lessons and from where I draw great strength. I love you all very much. I would also like to thank my husband who supported me despite the fact that he did not think I would ever complete this book.

To my best friend, Siobhan Norton, whose encouragement and belief in me allowed me to persevere and whose great sense of humor and late night sessions kept me laughing and sane. To me you are a bright star emanating light and love. What would I do without you?

To John Collins, from whom I have learned so much in such a short time. Thank you for your time and caring, for not pulling any punches, and for believing in me and in this book so intensely that you allowed me to believe in it myself.

To Mary Edwards, who gave me the encouragement to publish this book when I waivered and was unsure of my path.

I want to recognize Dawn, Laura, and Fiona from Flannery's Pub in Glasheen, Cork, Ireland for their warm welcomes, hilarious antics and fantastic cups of coffee. Thank you for letting me sit in the corner all day typing away on my computer. I can't tell you how much I appreciated your interest, your kindness, and your antics and sense of humor! You made writing fun.

Others who have helped me along my path to learning and understanding who I would like to thank and acknowledge are: Aiden Storey (my 1st Reiki Master & amazing psychic); Finnuala Conroy (my 2nd Reiki

Master); Tony Fitzpatrick (healer and kind human being); Richard Cooke (hypnotherapist/psychotherapist, author, and wonderful gentleman); Rosarie Dilworth (friend extraordinaire); Caroline Holohan, (gentle friend); Anne Ashley (colleague).

I want to recognize and thank Jacqueline Harvey (author & researcher) for taking time out of her busy schedule to read this book and to provide me with some critical edits and suggestions.

And last but not least, I would like to thank Pasty and George Conrades and their amazing children – Liza, Laura, Gus, Emma, and Anna – for all the love and support they extended to me so many years ago. I am a stronger and better person because of you.

Chapter 1

Introduction

The Beginning

It all began for me in January of the year 2000, when my son Emmet began sharing things with me that I could not explain. Had I been paying attention, I would now be setting the date even earlier, and I would be citing my son Connor as the one who forced me to think about what we narrowly define as reality, our capabilities, and about the activity that occurs all around us that the majority of us are unaware of, or dismiss out-of-hand. As a child, Connor, who was born with crystal-clear blue eyes (not the traditional murky-blue color most babies are born with), always attempted to communicate with me telepathically. I never appreciated this, finding it frustrating when I was trying to get an answer out of him or when I was trying to understand what he wanted from me. He would stare at me, full of expression and expectation. I would just patiently repeat the same question until he would sigh sadly and respond verbally. One day I remember saying to him, "I am not telepathic. I can't hear you in my head and I can't answer you that way. I'm sorry, but you'll just have to speak to me with your mouth and with words." His attempts to communicate with me telepathically ended shortly afterwards, and I have regretted my ignorance and impatience ever since. I am sure that had I asked him at the time, he would have taught me how to communicate that way, but I didn't and the result was that he repressed this natural gift.

Unfortunately for Connor, and for me, he was not able to explain or did not understand how to explain to me what he was able and attempting to do with me, and I was too ignorant and overwhelmed to realize that there was something special about this child that I could and should research and encourage him to develop. By the time Connor was obviously trying to communicate with me telepathically I had a new baby in my arms, his brother Emmet. I suppose there is no need to dwell in the past, and I have been assured that he could reactivate this ability should he ever choose to, but the point of sharing my experiences is to help others to learn from my errors and successes and to encourage parents to feel justified and empowered in knowing that their child is endowed with abilities that deserve the same consideration, respect, and support as, for example, a child that shows a tremendous aptitude for music, sports, or mathematics. All children come to us with special gifts and none should be discounted just because the establishment or our upbringing and experience do not recognize or understand them.

Emmet, unlike his brother, was not to be ignored. Being extremely verbal and interested in expressing and sharing things with me in a way that I could grasp, he forced me (kicking and screaming) to acknowledge that there was something unusual going on with him. The first time he shared anything with me was at the age of three and a half when he spoke of his "other mother" who was not from Earth and who had told him that he was different. I took note of it but was more amused than amazed by what he had said as I thought it was just a very clever way of him to sidestep the few rules we had in our house. However, quickly following that initial comment came one involving Jesus, and this one made me sit up and take notice. At the time that he told me about his discussion with Jesus he had not attended school or playschool, had not gone on any play dates, and did not watch TV as we only had videos and none of them were religious in nature. We did not attend church, being uncomfortable with organized religion. My husband was an Atheist and I was ambivalent at best. So for my child to suddenly begin speaking about a conversation with Jesus, or about Jesus at all, was shocking to me. I did not know what to think, and hoping that those around me may have experienced something similar or had heard of a child speaking in this way, I reached out to others and explained what Emmet had said. This was the first and one of the only times I shared information like this with other people until now. Responses ranged from "isn't that sweet" to suggestions that he was preordained to be a priest. Some said that perhaps God was trying to get my attention to direct me towards religion, while others just discounted it as a fluke. Not one person who knew the secular environment that my children were growing up in was able to explain how or why Emmet would have said what he did, and none of them appeared the least bit interested in trying to help me to figure it out. One person I know actually scoffed at me, suggesting that I didn't have enough to occupy myself with if I was concerned with Emmet's statement as, in their opinion, kids say the "weirdest" things and were not to be taken seriously. I felt very isolated and believed that I had exposed Emmet and myself unnecessarily by sharing this information with others. I vowed to be more guarded in the future and to find a way to educate myself without compromising any of us.

This is a situation that many parents find themselves in, especially if they are not associated with people and a community that is open-minded or "new-thought" in nature. Where do parents go for information? Who do they trust? These incidents involve the one thing that is the most precious in their lives and a parent does not want to expose their child to a misguided individual who may harm them in some way – either psychologically or emotionally – or who may provide no more insight into the situation than they could have determined themselves. Some other examples of the fairly useless information I received would include, "Oh, he/she is very psychic," or "Their third eye has just opened too fast, they will learn to manage it or close it down in time". It is very difficult, if a parent does not already have a circle of trusted friends who are capable of advising them, to reach out and trust others. Advice can also often involve money, which many parents do not have to spare on potentially wild-goose chases for information and advice that they may not necessarily agree with or know how to interpret and implement.

Another difficult aspect of dealing with a situation where your children appear to be psychic or are experiencing psychic events is that it is not usually a consistent occurrence. In other words, the child is not sharing experiences on a daily basis, and a long time can pass between statements. During this time, being human and being conditioned to discount and repress that which we find unsettling, we "forget". After a few days have passed where all "appears normal" we breathe a great sigh of relief and get on with our lives, placing the incident in a file that is deeply buried within our minds. It can also be difficult because psychic children are very guarded and may not open up when others are around, no matter how close those individuals may be to them, so that to the outside world they appear to be average, normal children. This was what occurred with Emmet and long periods passed before he would share another psychic insight or experience. There is, therefore, no guarantee that they will speak openly to another person about their abilities, even if the person you have located is both capable and interested in helping.

Yin & Yang

When Emmet first began to make unusual comments to me they were all about Jesus and angels, as I have said before. It was not until he began to see and experience terrifying things that I made any serious attempt at understanding what was occurring. As Emmet did not have a great command of the English language when he began to see monsters and demons, he had great difficulty finding the words to specifically describe his experiences. In desperation I turned to the only other medium of communication I could think of and asked him to draw what he had seen. This was positive in three ways, it helped me to understand what he was experiencing, it gave me a tangible journal for future reference, and it provided him with a love of art and creative expression that is a huge part of who he is and that continues to bring great joy and satisfaction into his life. I never projected my thoughts onto his drawings, I always took what he said to be fact even if I did not agree or understand. There were pictures he drew of entities which I did not find threatening but who he described as being horrible, while ones that I thought were upsetting he described as "helping" beings. So it is important that parents give their children the right to categorize and describe their pictures without question or edits.

As some of these initial drawings and explanations had biblical connotations, I brought some of the drawings that Emmet had done to a priest in a Catholic Church that was in the next town. The priest seemed interested as well as concerned due to the content of the pictures and asked to see Emmet who was asleep in his car seat in the car. I'm still not sure what he expected to see, but after looking at Emmet for a few seconds, and being visibly unimpressed, he shrugged and told me to contact him again if Emmet ever said anything else. Later on I went to speak to a Deacon who, to be fair, did try to help and to understand, but he was just not trained or capable of grasping what was happening or providing any advice. He did, however, bless our house. I thought it was so interesting that as he was leaving, Emmet became agitated and pointed out to him that he had not blessed the inside of two of the closets that were outside of his room. The deacon assured him that the house was "blessed enough" and that all would be well. Emmet was not convinced, and I have come to learn that they really should bless every space and corner in order to cleanse it properly. The result of the blessing was that some of the negative activity subsided for a time, but it did eventually recommence. I would consider that Emmet was correct, and that the closets should have been included in the blessing.

I should mention here that changing houses seems to make no difference at all, so you can save yourself the time, hassle, and money of moving. During the period of time when most of my children's psychic communications were occurring, we moved several times for unrelated reasons. It did not affect their abilities or experiences in any way nor cause them to subside.

Love, Understanding & No Fear

Some children are very communicative about what they are experiencing while others are not. I will not attempt to categorize any of them, as I find categorization restrictive and I don't like confining anyone within the parameters of a particular category. Children are all different and each of them is amazing in their own way. Some people generalize by saying, for example, that Indigo children are very expressive while Crystal children keep their information to themselves. This may well be true, but I am not an expert in this particular field and cannot definitively tell one from the other. I can tell you that both Indigo and Crystal children are considered to be deeply spiritual and sensitive. They are healers and are here to help us to affect positive change and get us onto the right path of growth and development.

Specifically, Indigo children can be described as Warrior Spirits whose auras (the energy field that surrounds any living thing) tend to have an unusual amount of Indigo blue in them. They are considered to be intelligent, psychic, and creative and are said to be here to shake us up on both a personal/individual and global/cultural level and force us to reevaluate our lives, systems, beliefs, traditions, cultures, behaviors, and priorities, among other things. In short, they are here to push us to re-examine and reassess our society beginning on an individual level and continuing upwards and outwards until all is encompassed. They have an extremely well-defined sense of justice and of right and wrong and will not back down easily – this is why they are called Warrior Spirits. Crystal children are described as being more even-tempered and calmer than the Indigos. They are also more sensitive and so are more easily hurt. Their primary task is to act as healers. So the Indigos come to shake things up and the Crystals follow to help us assimilate and heal.

But, in my opinion, what is more important than categorizing anyone is to acknowledge that children do have these amazing psychic and spiritual abilities and experiences. Keep in mind that just because a child, your child, has not shared any out-of-the-ordinary ideas or experiences with you does not mean that they are not having them; it just means that, for whatever reason, they are keeping things to themselves. All we can do as parents and carers is to provide a loving, supportive and open environment that gives them a safe space to do and experience what they need to - an environment that does not belittle new ideas or beliefs and that allows these children to flourish and to be who they are meant to be. All children require this for even the most basic development, but for a child who is experiencing psychic events, it is even more important. The reason for this is that society in general does not support psychic experiences and development. Both directly and indirectly, consciously and subconsciously, society works to repress and remove these abilities from the individual and pushes them towards linear thinking and an accepted mass-consciousness that is not altogether beneficial to our development as individuals or as a species. Psychic abilities are often portrayed as farcical or the product of mental illness and those who claim to posses them are depicted as charlatans or kooks. Our educational system forces children to stay in the here-and-now and to remain focused at all times. Children's natural tendency to allow their minds to wander is criticized and punished, or worse still they are medicated. The day-dreamer of old now becomes ADD or ADHD and must be dealt with accordingly. Society will not accept them. Children themselves will often make fun of peers who share their psychic knowledge as they have seen and heard their parents or others in positions of authority do, or because they have assimilated cues associated with attitudes towards psychic phenomena and psychics through the media. Children who are open about their psychic abilities learn quickly that there are very few places where they are safe to experience or to share their gifts, and little by little they close them down and become fully focused on the third-dimensional here-and-now reality that our society's restrictions in thinking and perception has created. It is therefore imperative that these children, all children, feel and know that their home is a sanctuary for them no matter what.

As for me, I can say that I have been successful in doing this at times, while I have failed miserably on occasion as is illustrated by Connor repressing his telepathic abilities due to my unsupportive reaction. Children who are attempting to express or explore their psychic talents and connections require patience and time, two things which are in short measure in this day and age. It is often difficult for adults to put into words what they have experienced psychically because words are so limiting and our points of reference here in the third dimension do not provide us with the verbiage, imagery, or references that are required to accurately explain what has been experienced in other realms or dimensions. It is doubly difficult for children who are only beginning to master a language; who may not understand that all of us cannot or perhaps never have experienced what they do; and who don't see their experiences as being out of the ordinary or unusual in any way. This idea that what these children are experiencing is ordinary and normal to them only occurred to me when I was questioning my daughter as to why she had not mentioned to me that she could see colors, or auras, around people. Her response came simply and quickly, "Because I thought everybody could see them." I had to laugh at myself when she shared this, and it may contribute to the reasons why many children don't mention psychic phenomena to us. For them, it's not psychic, it's normal! It is us, as individuals and as a society, who teach them that these things are not the "norm". So keep this in mind and also remember that even if you do try to do "all the right things", a child still may choose to shut down their psychic connections. This is not a failure. It is merely what the child feels they need to do or wants to do at that particular time. The important thing is that the child feels free to choose to remain open or closed, and that they are not pressured into choosing one option over the others by their loved ones.

Children are very sensitive to emotion and thought patterns, even emotion or thoughts that we attempt to hide, and so it is no good to pretend to be supportive or pleased about their psychic experiences if you, or others who spend a lot of time around your child, are internally screaming with fear, doubt, or derisive laughter. Children will know, they will sense it and for most of them their abilities will go into retreat. I say most of them, because there are exceptions to the rule, those who may go further into themselves and their otherworldly connections, immersing themselves in their gifts and their psychic experiences, but for the majority it is more likely that they will shut down, or switch off their psychic talents.

Fear is probably one of the worst reactions a person can have, and I know this from first-hand experience. The reason that fear is so dangerous is because it is a low-frequency emotion – it vibrates at a very low rate – and energy attracts like-energy to itself. So if a parent is feeling fearful about a child's abilities, they will most likely attract low or negative energy to the home and to a child who is psychically aware and sensitive and, therefore, more vulnerable to this energy. As silly as this sounds now, when my son Emmet began to talk about Jesus and wrote what I refer to as scrolls, because he rolled them up like a scroll when he was done writing them, I panicked. I went from mild amusement to interest to panic. I panicked for a multitude of reasons, all of them stupid and much of the fear I harnessed came from outside sources. I feared that these communications meant something "big" for him, that I needed to help him to learn and achieve something that I could not even begin to fathom and had no knowledge about. I feared that this would mean a miserable life or a horrific death – let's not forget that historically so many of those who have claimed to work for the Divine or to communicate with the Light have not met with easy lives or happy endings. I was worried that perhaps Emmet was not communicating with entities of Light but of the Dark who were leading him to believe that they were good. I thought and feared many things, none of which were valid or had any worth. The result of these internal fears and my brooding upon them was that Emmet went from engaging those of the Light to being terrified on a regular basis by monsters and frightening beings. His experience went from that of peace and joy to one of utter terror, and opened him up to psychic attacks. He became so open that one attack was able to manifest physically and left him so bruised that I took him to see his doctor. My fear produced and drew similar energy to my home. My fear attracted distorted beings to us. My unspoken fear changed Emmet's experience from one of joy and love to one of dread, and he too then began to fear, further feeding the low energy in the house and giving more power to negative entities to access him. But as there is nothing that goes wrong that cannot be corrected, I prayed (something that was extremely unusual for me at the time) and asked for help, handing the problem to God and God took care of it. The "monsters" no longer troubled him as they had been doing, and I learned to relax. As I relaxed and my fear dissipated, the number of negative experiences that Emmet was having subsided considerably and the intensity diluted so that while he was still able to see things that frightened him, they were not able to physically harm him or interact with him in the same manner. So this is not to say that if you feel no fear that a psychically aware child will not see "monsters", they very well may. If they can see beyond the veil, they can see all the entities, both benevolent and malevolent, that originate from and inhabit many other dimensions. But without fear as part of the equation negative and misguided beings will be less likely to be drawn to them, and the child's energy will resonate at a higher level, which in and of itself provides protection. Very simply, in a home where fear is absent these entities will not have the same ability to interfere as they would otherwise.

Sit In A State Of-Love

We are most alive, closest to the beautiful and amazing beings we truly are, when we sit in love because we are then living in our hearts. The heart is the very center of our being because it is Love and, therefore, it is the key to All because, I believe, that within our dimension Love is the highest expression and best use of the pure energy that we consider to be God, the Source, True Consciousness, or however you feel comfortable describing "It".

It is simple to go to our hearts, but we make it difficult to remain there by allowing our focus to become overwhelmed by the distractions of our world and, more importantly, for our attention to be drawn to the (often negative) internal banter of our minds. There is a constant struggle between the heart and the head that we allow and that we create every day. We are already perfect but we cloud this reality with disbeliefs and mis-beliefs. We then further cement and reinforce this skewed reality by strengthening it with negative emotions. Emotion gives power, great power, to thoughts. One without the other has little effect. Separately they are like ripples in a pond. But to combine the two is to call upon our Power of Creation which, despite what many of us think, is mighty indeed especially if our thoughts and emotions are combined with those of others. We can use this Power of Creation in a positive or a negative way. The choice is ours.

There are only two states of being and acting: Of-Love and Not-of-Love. Think about this for a minute - all human emotion and actions can be placed in one of these two categories as they are all the fruit of one state or the other. Kindness and charity come from being in a state Of-Love, while jealously and violence, or any action or emotion that is an attempt to control, are spawned from being in a state that is Not-of-Love. We need for our sake, and for the sakes of our children, to turn away from being in a state that is Not-of-Love and do our best to maintain the perfect state Of-Love. It is not that difficult to reach this state but the challenging part is remaining there. It requires that we reevaluate and often unlearn what we have been taught by others and have accepted to be true about ourselves and about our environment and we must analyze our thoughts and opinions to see which have validity and which do not hold true for us anymore. We must break our habit of defaulting, without thinking, to being focused on distracting or misplaced priorities in order to maintain a higher vibration and state of being by creating and sustaining a positive state of mind. It requires us to learn to love ourselves and forgive ourselves for the things that we have done and for those that we have failed to do, as well as to forgive others in our lives who have hurt or failed us. All of this is part of the long-term efforts that we need to make in order to sit in a state Of-Love easily and be able to maintain it more consistently. So we begin with little steps and one of the best first steps I can think of is attaining, if only for a moment, that state so that you can experience how marvelous, uplifting, and emancipating it is so that you can understand in a real way what you are striving for.

So how do you get into this state Of-Love? My friend, Irish psychic and medical intuitive, John Collins showed me a very simple yet effective method. Take a minute now and close your eyes, taking a few deep breaths to clear your mind and to help you to relax. Bring your attention or awareness to the center of your chest where your heart chakra is located. (A chakra is a medium through which we release and take in vital energy. There are seven major ones that are aligned with the center-line of the body, or the spine, starting with one on the top of your head known as the Crown Chakra. They are sometimes depicted as flowers, wheels, or whirling vortexes.) Now think of a person or situation that fills your heart with love and joy. Focus on and hold that feeling. When you feel that it is glowing within your chest, allow it to spread throughout your being and let it engulf you and infuse your senses. Again, hold this feeling and you have done it. For practice, try doing this before you make a difficult decision or deal with a challenging situation or person, or project that feeling towards something or someone that is causing you upset. Sit in a state Of-Love first and then surround the problem person or situation with this love and then release that person, problem or challenge. Try doing it randomly throughout the day and you will find that as it becomes more automatic you will be able to hold the state for longer and longer periods of time.

Children can and should be taught to do this, especially psychic children. They are so surrounded and bombarded by negative energy, images, thoughts, and actions of others that they need to understand how they can return to their true state where they vibrate at their optimum level. At this level, not only will they feel better and function more effectively, they will also be more protected as their own auras will vibrate properly and so will become more impenetrable. They will also be better able to access higher and protective energy and beings whenever they have a need, whether consciously or subconsciously. There is absolutely no down side to being in a state Of-Love.

We have both the ability and the responsibility to change, and it is not as difficult as many of us make it out to be. When I look at the example of Jesus, it seems to me that when you boil it down to the very basics about what he lived to illustrate, it is that all we need to do is to go into our hearts, sit in and maintain the state Of-Love, and forgive ourselves and others. By doing this you free yourself of everything that you have bound yourself with and you become empowered through this freedom. You also free and empower others through forgiveness. Love yourself and others, forgive and be forgiven. (I use Jesus in this example because I know more about him and am therefore most comfortable offering my opinion on this matter in relation to his life and teachings. I fully recognize that he is not the only teacher who has come to us to show us these truths and to lead by example.)

As Emmet grew older, he spoke less and less about unusual things as his abilities changed tact and became more of what I would call intuition and insightfulness. He seemed to be able to just "plug-in" to the Universe and speak a truth or express an understanding of something that was well beyond his years, exposure, or experience. One day he said to me, "It's not that I don't want my gifts, I am just taking a break right now. I just want to be normal and do fun things. I'll get back to them when I am ready." And that was that. All the angst and distress and worry I expended for absolutely no reason. Emmet, like all children, is the one in control of his path and in charge of his abilities. The best we can do is to try to create an environment that allows them to make whatever decisions they want or need to make when it is right for them to do so.

Keep a Record

So, when does this all begin for a child? When does it end? How do you know if your child is experiencing psychic phenomena? What do you do? I can do no more than to share my experiences because I don't believe that any of this can be defined as each child is different, but many people have reported that most children's ability to see and interact with beings and other phenomena begins to subside between the ages of seven and nine. As I said before, I missed the mark entirely with my first born and made some very stupid errors with my second. Take heart in that there is always help just one prayer away, and that God, knowing we are only human, built safeties into the system. Errors require correction and forgiveness (this includes forgiving yourself), and the willingness to try again to get things right, but nothing else. If we find that we are not living in a state Of-Love, then we merely need to shift back into it. It is so simple that it can be hard to accept, but this is the truth. I have explained how I made mistakes with my children, but I also rectified the situation to the best of my ability and learned as I went. I tried to let them know that I was open to anything they wanted to tell me, that I would never belittle them, and that I would always believe them even when I found it difficult to do so. I also insured that they understood to the very core of their being that they were loved unconditionally. This carried a lot of weight with them and despite my foul-ups they continued to share with me then and they still do so today.

One of the things that I always did, and which I recommend to anyone whose children are sharing these types of events with them, is to keep a record of what they have said, experienced, done, or drawn. These are invaluable for future reference for you and your child and can be helpful when similar or related events or messages come through. It also illustrates to the child that you see value in what they are sharing, and this serves to strengthen the bond of trust and openness. My husband had a great deal of difficulty accepting or being involved in any way with what the children were experiencing on this level. He never voiced any criticism to them when they were young, but he merely made himself inaccessible when it came to psychic topics. They knew this without ever being told and, in fact, recognized and accepted this fact before I did. When Emmet was four and had shared what he called his "last time secret with Jesus" with me (see Chapter 2) I asked him if he would tell his father about it. His response was that he would not. When I asked why, he replied very pragmatically, "Because he wouldn't believe me." It did not seem to bother Emmet that his father would not believe him, he just did not wish to engage his father in this manner knowing that he would be met with unspoken disbelief. I also think that he did not feel that my husband was ready, and he seemed to know that this was something that needed to be respected. We all develop and understand various concepts and truths at different times and Emmet, even at that young age, appeared to understand that this type of development was not to be forced.

Another thing that I can recommend is emphasizing that everyone's opinion is valid and that each person, especially within the family unit, has the right to hold their own beliefs as long as these beliefs do not involve harm in any form. This gives a child tremendous room to express their thoughts and ideas without restricting them to any point-of-view. In my house there are varying opinions on the topic of what is real and true and everyone is expected to respect the opinions of the other even when they don't agree with each other. This code was breached only once from within the family unit and it was met with utter disdain by the children. The conflict was quickly rectified and the person who had been urged to scoff apologized and recognized the right of the others to believe in whatever they wanted to. So being homogeneous in familial beliefs is not a goal, but respect is.

The Psychic Connection

Psychic connections and communication between parent and child are always present, it is up to us to be open to them and accept them. I believe my psychic connection with my children began years before they were even conceived. One of my best friends and I were talking about children. For no reason that I could think of I suddenly had the urge to tell her that I would have two boys and a girl in that order; that the two boys would be eighteen months apart, while the girl would arrive two-and-a-half years later; that their eyes would be different colors (blue, brown, and green); and that if I had any more they would be twins. All of what spontaneously came through me that night proved correct except that I was never blessed with the opportunity to find out about the twins as we did not go beyond three children.

When I was pregnant with Emmet, I suddenly felt strongly that the umbilical cord was wrapped around his neck. I made an appointment to go see my doctor in order to explain this and see what could be done. She was very dismissive and obviously did not take me seriously, putting it down to pre-birth nerves. I was angry when I left the office, but I allowed her "informed" opinion to override mine, and I came to feel that all was well. It wasn't until Emmet was being born that this thought jumped back into my head with a tremendous force. In a panic I reminded the doctor to check the umbilical cord which she did. She ordered me not to push under any circumstances while she attempted to cut the cord. Afterwards the doctor told me that the cord had been wrapped around his neck several times.

These are examples of being connected prior to birth, examples of this post-birth connection could fill a book itself. However, I will share another experience that occurred with my daughter, Anithe, directly after birth. She had just been born and I was sitting up looking at her. The nurse placed her down between my feet and removed her hand to grab a towel. I was not aware that the nurse was going to let go of Anithe (something that was inconceivable), and the time between the nurse removing her hand and what occurred next was infinitesimally small. For reasons I cannot explain, I grabbed for her before I even realized that there was a need. I moved so quickly that I was not even aware of what I was doing until after the event. Simultaneously as I reached for her, the nurse removed her hand from Anithe as she turned to quickly grab a towel, and Anithe rolled - something that shocked all of us. Had I not grabbed for her at that exact moment she would have ended up on the floor of the delivery room and it would not have been a happy ending. So this psychic connection is very real and is very helpful to say the least.

Having a psychic connection with your child does not mean that you are "a psychic". It merely means that you have moments of "knowing" that relate to your children. Most mothers possess this ability, and it is these psychic moments that are often the reason that any child survives beyond the age of four! It is useful for many things, such as knowing when your child is in danger, is ill, or is having difficulty in their lives. It is equally useful when a child does share a psychic insight or experience as it helps you to know that it is real – that your child is telling the truth. And this is extremely important: no one, no matter who they are, will know better than a connected parent, or a parent who is in tune with their child, what that child is really experiencing. No one else will know your child as well as you or will have the benefit of the inner understanding and the psychic and emotional connections that you have with your child. You may not have the ability to actively participate in what they are experiencing but you will know that what they are sharing is true and is as real as anything else the rest of us perceive. Trust yourself.

The fact that what children are sharing with us is real and not fantasy is an important point. We must remember that we have been conditioned and indoctrinated as we developed into the adults by our families and our communities. Much of what we accept as truth was constructed over time by those who have had a desire for power and to control, or who have been misguided. The tools they have used in constructing a system of belief have often been fear, and they preyed upon our indoctrinated fear and respect of power or authority. We relinquish great personal power when we accept the reality and truths of others **without question**, and it is time that we become brave enough to question these "truths" and learn to open our minds to other possibilities and explanations. We can no longer allow ourselves to be boxed in by the narrow and self-serving definitions of reality and truth that has been constructed for us by others who have an agenda, especially when these ideas and beliefs are being challenged by the one group of people who we know, who we trust, and who have absolutely nothing to gain by sharing with us – our children.

This is a difficult challenge because our system of belief is what we are comfortable with. It defines us and associates us with a larger social group and it is the cornerstone from which we launch ourselves into the world. We have been taught that it is the map that allows us to navigate through this life we are experiencing here and now. Modifying or altering our belief system rocks and shakes up our world and the world of those who are around us. Resistance rears its head in many forms from many different areas of the social structure and it can really only be defined in two words – bullying and control, both of which are fear-based. The belief is that the status quo must be maintained and it is often those who believe that they are motivated by love and think they are protecting us who are really only protecting themselves. For when you challenge your own belief system, you are also challenging the belief system of those who are in the same camp as you once were and this can be a threat. One of the main ways that resistance manifests itself is through ridicule and the threat of being ostracized. These are both fear-based tools, and while they are low-level energies they gain tremendous strength because they are multiplied each time you encounter them or fear them. It can take great personal strength to face this challenge but it is a challenge that must be met if we are to grow and progress. This is a challenge that should be faced even if in the end a person returns to the belief system they originally began with. At least they are then accepting a belief system from a position of independent thought. As I began to open myself up to various ideas and concepts I found that there were ideas which I initially accepted, only to discard them later and those that I discounted at first only to embrace as time went on. This is a path of development and growth. Nothing needs to be set in stone other than the willingness to consider with an open mind the possibilities of other definitions of what reality is, of what is true and real.

Another form that resistance can take is arrogance, again a fear-based defense and a very effective one as it carries with it a sometimes unspoken but thoroughly communicated attitude that anyone who questions the norm or who accepts alternative truths is a little short on intelligence or is unbalanced and socially unacceptable in some way. Pointing to similar-minded learned people or to the multitudes of those who accept a certain system of beliefs, they scoff at the idea that anyone, let alone children, could possibly provide greater insights or have a deeper understanding of the truth than the time-tested systems that are already in place. This is a manifestation of the conscious mind, of the ego speaking, and those who function purely from this platform cannot fathom the connection or the messages that children spontaneously share.

A Knowing

Most people have been taught that babies are Tabula Rasa – empty slates waiting to be written upon by their parents and by society - and certainly, in relation to this world and this dimension, in terms of our societies with their rules and beliefs, this is true. But I believe that children come to us with a great amount of insight and understanding, a deep knowing and a connection to the Source that can explain what is true and real. These truths, this "knowing" is often revealed in small observations and comments, fleeting gems of knowing that can appear fantastical but are genuine and valid. I use the term "knowing" instead of knowledge to describe what our children can share with us, because that is really what it is. They have not spent years of research and study trying to find the truths that they share, they merely know with every fiber of their being that what they are saying is correct and true. When we open ourselves up to this knowing and the precious information that children are willing to share with us we are touched and comforted, for we too know in our hearts that this is not fantasy.

There are those who will point to the fact that some of the imagery or the source of the messages and experiences are not consistent, that they vary. They use this as a way of undermining the message and the concepts that are coming through children. They point to these inconsistencies as a way of "proving" that they are not real. It must be remembered that all information that comes from the Universe comes through the filter that is the individual themselves, and therefore the information is influenced by the person or the environment that the person is in. So a child from a Christian family will speak of Jesus and relate Christian symbols and references, while a child from another background will communicate information that is in line with their religious and cultural beliefs, or the beliefs of their communities. It is of the utmost importance to recognize that it is the deeper meaning of the message that is important, not the symbolic trappings that it comes in. For it is here that the truth of the messages, the knowledge and the lessons that we need to learn lie. Most messages communicate the idea that we are not alone; that we must never fear for there is no need; that we should love and allow ourselves to be loved by each other and by the Source; that we all come from God and that we carry that light-energy within us; that we are all one and that we have free will. These are the points and messages we should focus on and take to heart.

I want to make it very clear that my children are not unusual in what they have experienced, although they may be unusual in terms of how much of their experiences they have shared. They are no different than any other child and are no better behaved or better prepared for life on the Earth than anyone else. They have their ups and downs, their good days and their bad. They do not sit around discussing the meaning of life or meditating on their spare time. They play games (and have been known to cheat at times), they swear when they think I am out of ear shot, their table manners require constant correction, they eat meat and love sweet things. They can be moody and selfish at times or they can be kind, loving and giving of themselves.

Many people, including family members who know them and have spent regular time with them are completely unaware that this ability, this psychic awareness, exists because up until now my children have chosen not to share this aspect of themselves with others. I point this out because there can be a misperception, one which I held at one point, that being connected to the Universe, to the Divine, would somehow rub off and cause the child to become more perfect, less fraught with human failings. This is simply not true. For the most part the human failings and limitations live side-by-side with their understanding of the Light and their ability to tap into it without any thought or effort. We have been mislead by examples of a minority of young children who are considered to be highly evolved, and to behave accordingly, to believe that this is what we should expect if our children are really and truly communicating psychically with higher beings. This is an unrealistic expectation. The point is that all children are, on some level, communicating with higher beings and beings from other dimensions, we just don't often realize it, and "good" or mature behavior is not indicative of this type of communication one way or the other. We all come down here to experience this plane, this amazing and challenging place we call Earth. Everyone has different abilities to deal with these challenges, and some take longer to assimilate the energies and lessons down here than others. Some never get off the starting line. You cannot judge the psychic abilities or connections that a child has based on their day-to-day behavior for it is not a litmus test of anything greater. It just is what it is.

In fact, I could argue that being psychic and more aware and sensitive to both positive and negative energies and beings could cause a child to have more extreme emotional swings than those children that are not as sensitive. Remember, we are all Beings of Light who vibrate at a very high level, who were brave enough to enter into a very dense dimension with huge limitations, constrictions, and restrictions. This alone can be overwhelming. Add to this the fact that these children can pick up the thoughts and feelings of those around them and are open to negative energies and entities, and the fear and frustration must be enormous at times. Often they are not even aware that they are picking up negativity from outside themselves and cannot, therefore, make a parent aware of the situation. They merely feel as if they are being dragged down or overwhelmed emotionally and energetically. Their moods change and they can, in some cases, lash out in an attempt to release the pent up negativity. In these situations, as difficult as it may be, parents and guardians should attempt to approach the child and the situation with love. It is fast, efficient, and allows the child to recalibrate themselves in a positive way. I have found that approaching my children when they are agitated, holding them in an embrace and telling them that I love them before we deal with what they may have done and why, immediately diffuses the negativity and returns them to a state Of-Love. Everything calms down and they are usually the ones who offer up what transpired. They provide explanations as to certain situations developed that are always much deeper and insightful that anything I could have guessed at. Every time I do not approach a situation with them with love, I always regret it and it always takes much longer to rectify as there are hurt feelings and resentment that linger on. Situations can always be healed, so if you don't begin dealing with a situation with love, you can always reach for it at any time when dealing with children. They usually respond immediately.

We are odd creatures. Parents whose children may be espousing psychic messages and experiencing psychic events are often perplexed and frightened by them, while those who have children who appear not to be expressing psychic insight may be concerned or feel that somehow their child is lacking. This is not a competition and we must remember that all children express things differently and at different times in their lives. What is even more important to remember is that just by being here, just by their presence here on Earth, all children are helping to change and raise the vibration of those around them and of the planet. This is why they have come.

Love is All

The main purpose of this book - the motivation for sharing my experiences and insights about my children with everyone who is interested - is to help parents and those who work with children who demonstrate unusual or psychic abilities to understand that these abilities are not figments of their imagination, nor are they things to be repressed or feared. They are natural and they are gifts that will benefit us all – these children are here to help us and to teach us. I can honestly say that while the experiences of parents of these psychic children can be incredibly challenging and difficult at times, we benefit tremendously and develop and grow in ways that could never be imagined. I have met so many wonderful people and have learned so much over the last eight years and I am humbled and appreciate the gifts that have been given to me so freely.

My children have taught me. They opened doors for me and I walked through them, though sometimes reluctantly, and even when what I experienced was fear, there was always the lesson of love, support and understanding that came with it and that balanced it out and made me a better person. If nothing else I have learned that beyond a shadow of a doubt the only real thing is love, and if we all work from that base, no matter how difficult, there is nothing that we cannot accomplish. This is what these children have come to teach us – love is strength, love is all.

What's In This Book

This book covers many of the individual experiences that my children shared with me over the years exactly as they were communicated. Nothing has been removed except where I felt that the information was too personal to my children. Also included is a hypnosis session that I held with my eldest son, Connor, in 2008 about an experience he had shared with me eight years earlier and one that I held with my daughter, Anithe, three years after she had experienced an alien visit. Pictures are included but are all in black and white as color was not an option for the printing of this book. You can view the pictures my children drew in color, as well as photographs of activity around them and our house either on my website www.aknowing.com or on my **Facebook** page *A Knowing – Living with Psychic Children*. You can also reach me through both venues with any questions or comments you may have or through my email - chris@aknowing.com.

Chapter 2

Jesus and the Angelic

Children can experience the Divine without ceremony or preparation partly because they are so open to it. They have not yet learned that they are not supposed to be able to reach out to or be contacted by those of the Light. For obvious reasons, these are the experiences that I enjoy hearing about the most. Among other things, children are here to give us hope and remind us of how brightly our light can shine if we would only allow it to. It is a lesson I am still learning, and I am thankful that I have been given such wonderful teachers.

Initially part of the difficulty I had accepting and understanding what was being communicated through my children was the fact that there was always only enough information coming through to get my attention and to cause me to be flooded with confusion, and never enough to provide me with the answers…or so it seemed to me at the time. The other problem is that I am very literal, which is one of the reasons that the symbolic references that my children often shared baffled me. I was always ***afraid*** (note the terminology) that I would misunderstand the symbols and get things wrong which, ironically, was the only obstacle that stood in my way of understanding! I did not trust myself, I did not trust the messages or the source of the messages, and I did not trust that on a deep level my children understood what they needed to without "expert" help. They didn't need me or anybody else to explain anything to them or to do anything about what they were experiencing. In fact, it seems that part of the reason they were sharing all of this with me was so that ***I*** would and could grow in my trust in the Source and in the Universe and to jump-start my personal journey of searching for answers, understanding, and knowing on a spiritual level that I had put off for so long. So should you have doubts about what you should be doing in these circumstances, my advice is to surround yourself and your family with love, trust your children, learn to trust yourself and your intuition, and open your eyes and your heart and begin your own quest of learning and growing.

In Jesus' Tummy

The first experience I had with any of my children referring to contact with, or knowledge of, Jesus or Beings of Light came in January 2000. My son, Emmet, was four years old when he shared this with me. One aspect that immediately concerned me was the warning of potential danger and violence within the message. As he had not attended school, did not watch unsupervised TV, and did not go on play dates, I could not imagine where the concept of such "bad" people could have come from. This communication came to Emmet in the form of a "dream" or rather this is how he referred to this interaction.

*"Connor and Anithe (his brother and sister) were in **your** tummy, Mommy, and I was in Jesus' tummy. Jesus spoke to me and told me about bad things, especially bad men who might hurt me. Jesus told me he would protect me but...I have to be careful. They can sneak in at night, take me away, and cut me up! I have to be careful so that they can't hurt me." –E*

I think anyone reading this can understand why it concerned me beyond the fact that I was completely bewildered as to where this concept and topic of Jesus came from, let alone an adult Jesus. As I explained in Chapter 1, at that time our house was a neutral house in terms of religion and the only mild reference my children had been exposed to in terms of the existence of anyone named "Jesus" was a child in a manger at Christmas whose birthday it was. They knew more about Rudolf the Red-Nosed Reindeer and Frosty the Snowman than Jesus, Mary, and Joseph. So confusion was part of my internal reaction and serious concern was the other.

While the men in this dream could have been human or alien beings who could literally "cut him up", I have come to believe otherwise. I think that instead they represented the fact that Emmet can sense, and sometimes see, what others are feeling or what is occurring in their lives, and this can cause him distress. So people (men) could hurt Emmet unwittingly just through everyday thoughts and emotions that were completely unrelated to him. The other part of this is that because at that time he was so open psychically, he could see and experience many of the not-so-pleasant entities that are around us and, yes, they could frighten him and try to cause him harm.

It was the "can hurt me" aspect that I focused on and not the most beautiful part of this dream in which Jesus assured Emmet that He would be protecting him. What an amazing gift of reassurance and love! Instead, by focusing on the negative aspect of the dream I brought fear in around Emmet. I should have had the faith and the trust to have recognized this promise to my son, and I should have felt great love, peace, and honor that this protection had been promised to Emmet, but this is not how I responded.

It is so easy in this world and in this reality that we have created for ourselves to focus on the negative, to lock onto the fear, because we are surrounded by it – our society is based upon it. Our conscious minds have been trained to scan the horizon for danger and to live off-balance, perpetually concerned about protecting ourselves and our loved ones from danger. It is much harder to look at a promise of love and believe in it because we have constructed a world in which love can seem a rare truth and trust is often abused. The days of, "I give you my word of honor" are long gone, although they can always be recaptured if enough of us desire it. And so, I did not trust, even though this promise was given to my son by one whose trust I would never question.

In terms of Emmet protecting himself and being careful, this referred to an emotional and psychic protection. Emmet needed to be in an environment that was safe and supportive and that surrounded him with love. When a child, or anybody for that matter, is in an environment Of-Love and can sit in a place Of-Love, their energy will vibrate at a higher level. This higher level of vibration is a protection, as entities and people who vibrate at a lower rate must either raise their own vibration, thus improving and growing, or they must leave. (There is also another option, which is covered in Chapter 5.)

The image or symbolism of Emmet being in Jesus' tummy was another stumbling block for me, although in the end the answer was quite simple. Emmet feels closely associated to Jesus on a Soul Level and Emmet's light or energy vibration is gold, a color that is attributed to Jesus and is referred to as Christ Light. This is not to say that children who vibrate at this level will behave in a Christ-like manner! It merely means that when he is at his best, when he can sit in a state Of-Love and not be dragged down by negative energy and emotion, he resonates at the frequency of gold Christ Light.

Missing Jesus

All remained quiet until March 6th, 2000, and so I had decided to discount the first incident as an inexplicable fluke. As I was to discover, it was merely the tip of the iceberg in a long series of "inexplicable flukes" that continued on for years. On March 6th Emmet again spoke to me of Jesus. Unfortunately, he chose a moment when we were crossing a rather busy and loud road and I was unable to hear some of the words. He refused to repeat or explain his statement. As you will read from my comments, I was not very supportive - a mistake I never made with him or any of my children again. I am only grateful that this display of doubt on my part did not deter Emmet from continuing to share with me. It does not come across in the text (although I have added the spirit in which some of my statements were made in order to better convey my attitude) but I was fairly frustrated and exacerbated by this subject coming up again.

"I'm very sad mommy, I miss Jesus." –E

"Jesus is always with you love."- CP (exasperated)

*"**No!** I really miss him!"* -E

"How could you possibly miss him Emmet? You've never been with him!"- CP (annoyed)

"Yes I have! I was with him before I was in your tummy. He was very nice and said nice things to me." -E

"What kind of nice things?" –CP (perplexed and now interested)

"He told me he would protect me and that I would be a (word inaudible). I will get rid of (word inaudible) and kill a dragon, and then the world will be a better place. Mommy, why do we have to die to go and be with God when we were with Him already before?" -E

    As if I was not confused enough by this sudden explosion of Jesus in our lives, Emmet later referred to this experience as his "last time secret with Jesus", a statement he would not expound on, and spoke of having been taken often by Jesus to the "desert house".
    For me, the most amazing part about this statement was the fact that he felt that we had come from God and had already been with Him before our earthly incarnations. More than anything else, it was this amazing concept that really grabbed my attention and caused me to attempt in vain to get him to repeat what he had said so that I could hear the missing words. In retrospect I feel that those words which I did not catch were not for me to hear. They probably would have sent me into a tail-spin and I would have put pressure on myself and on Emmet to do certain things in order to be sure that he accomplished what he came here to do. This would not have been good for Emmet. After years of brow-beating myself for not listening well enough I have come to the conclusion that **he was inspired to share this with me at exactly that moment in time because I was not able to fully focus on him or hear all that he was saying.** I believe that whatever his task is, he will accomplish it as long as he has the sup-

port and confidence in himself and is surrounded by love. Beyond that, I need not worry. Also, as I said in Chapter 1, these children change the world just by being here and bringing their vibrations to the Earth. Emmet may never have to "do" anything as long as he can maintain his energy and vibration, as his mere presence may be all that is required of him. The other part of this message that was important for me to understand is that Emmet is protected. In this, Jesus reiterated to him that He would protect Emmet, and I feel Emmet shared this with me in order to give me confidence. It took many years for me before this truth sunk in and I finally released the fear completely.

Jesus' Picture

From March 10th, Emmet began to have terrible nightmares every night. He also still spoke of Jesus, continuing to wonder where he was, a question I could not answer because in my mind, Jesus is "there" and we are "here", although I eventually settled on using the idea that Jesus resided in his heart, a theme my other two children grabbed onto as well. It never occurred to me that Emmet could easily access and communicate with Jesus at any "time" and from any "place" because Emmet did not recognize or acknowledge the separation that I did. For him, as with most children, all was and is connected. There is no veil. I never encouraged him to attempt to directly access Jesus and, in fact, probably contributed to him believing that he was powerless to do so. As I have grown in understanding I realize that there is no "here" or "there", there only "is". There are no barriers except for the ones we construct and accept as reality. And this is where the parent becomes such an integral part of these children's development and in the construction of their ideas concerning their abilities and limitations and in relation to the "structure" of our reality. If we assure them that they cannot reach out, or that we are separated and alone, then this is what our children will incorporate into their reality and that is how they will feel and see the world – separate and alone. If we teach them that All-is-One, that there is no separation, and that they can indeed interact with the Divine at any time, then this is what they will believe. So we can limit and constrict our children or we can empower and free them.

As Emmet had difficulty describing what he was experiencing at the time, I asked him to draw what he saw. He sat down, totally focused, and produced eleven pictures, describing each one as he drew and handed them to me. He would then turn back to continue with his drawing. I did not question him until he had completed his drawings. The first drawing he did was of Jesus. At first glance I was confused to see wings and an oval drawn down his center, as well as what I mistakenly thought was short hair (he corrected me saying it was a crown of flowers), but no beard. I felt that this couldn't be Jesus. I thought that perhaps it was some other angelic being that Emmet had confused with Jesus somehow. I asked him if he was sure that this picture was of Jesus and Emmet was adamant that it was.

Jesus

To see a clearer copy go to www.aknowing.com or to the Facebook page: A Knowing-Living with Psychic Children

It wasn't until a few years later when I saw a depiction of a soul in the Astral Plane that matched Emmet's depiction of Jesus that this drawing made sense - Emmet had drawn the energy fields that surround the spiritual/astral body. I am ashamed to admit that I was more impressed by what he had drawn **after** I found the artistic impression of a soul on the Astral Plane, than I had been when Emmet first handed this drawing to me. Seeing the other drawing gave me an explanation of what Emmet had drawn in terms of the "wings", the "oval" and the "crown of flowers", and provided me with a validation that I should not have required, but did. The reason for my doubts when I first saw Emmet's drawing was based on my preconception, my limited concept of what was real and how things should appear. As this drawing did not look the way I have been taught Jesus should look, I could not accept it as being valid, real, or true. It wasn't until I saw the other drawing of an Astral-Plane entity that I realized what the energy fields around Jesus were and how accurately Emmet had depicted them in his drawing.

Jesus' Visit

My eldest son, Connor, shared his experience of a visit from Jesus with Emmet and me on May 17, 2000. This is one of the only experiences that Connor has ever vocalized. He was seven years old at the time. This was one of the most moving experiences that has ever been shared with me partly because of the emotion with which he communicated it. It is this sincerity and intensity of emotion that a parent will pick up on and should always trust. Children often become very animated when they discuss these psychic experiences and communicate them with an intensity of emotion that stands out from the normal expression of excitement, and a parent will recognize this. If you are looking for a key to knowing when to listen and take them seriously, emotional intensity is a good barometer.

Being specific and insisting on accuracy is another. Children often will not allow you to alter or bend what they are reporting to fit into your reality or society's preconceptions of what things are or should be. They know what they have experienced and see no reason why anyone should want to modify it or adapt it for any reason. They don't care if it does not match someone else's experience because they are only interested in sharing their experience. And this brings me to a very important point that my son, Connor, explained to me. Everything is energy. We perceive and process energy to make sense of it, but each of us processes it in a slightly different way based on beliefs, expectations, spiritual advancement…in short, what we are comfortable with. This variation amongst us in relation to perceiving energy is heightened when we perceive things outside of the Third Dimension because we process this energy in the way that we are most comfortable with, and many of us are comfortable with different things and different realities. There is no "right way" to perceive this energy. So if two people are viewing the same plane one may describe it to be very much like Earth while the other may see it as otherworldly because that is how each of them is comfortable accepting it. It works the same way with entities, and so two people can be sensing or seeing the same entity but may perceive it differently. It does not mean that one person is right and the other is wrong, or that they are not viewing the same place or thing. It merely means that they are each comfortable processing the energy-input in different ways. So it is with the little child that reports what they have experienced. They have perceived something in a certain way and cannot understand the need for anyone else to require it to conform to the way others have depicted similar experiences, places, or entities. For the child, it is what it is.

An aspect of this story that struck me was the fact that Connor said that he had wanted to go and stay with Jesus, something that would have been extremely unusual for him as it was so out of character, and so was another indicator that he had experienced something extremely unusual. Connor, at the time, hated to leave my side so his comments about wanting to stay with Jesus and not return to us gave merit to his description of the event. I have no way of knowing exactly when this visit took place as Connor chose not to share it immediately. He was prompted to share this information in order to try to console his brother after Emmet had observed a frightening entity making its way through our upstairs landing while we were cuddled up reading a bedtime story. (The information regarding the entity that Emmet saw is contained in Chapter 5.)

"I had a dream the other Friday, but it wasn't a dream…it was real. I was asleep, but it really happened. I know because Jesus is in my heart." -C

"What was the dream about?" -CP

"Jesus came (to me) and was by my bed. He had brown hair and a brown mustache and a ring of light around his head...he told me about the Dream and the Sky Police. They are angels. They are everywhere. They protect us. He told me about the different cities where angels live up in Heaven. There is an angel that stands at every door to make sure nothing bad gets in. I wanted to go with him, but he told me that I couldn't go with him there until I die. Oh Mommy, there was so much beautiful light (around him), and I felt so happy and...so safe. I just wanted to go with him. Then Jesus told me to be very, very good and never to lie. Because, when you lie you help Lucifer. I promised him I would try. He promised me that he would come and visit me again, but he hasn't yet...Mommy, if you try to be good, but make mistakes, Jesus understands doesn't he?" -C

There is so much in this short description to provide hope and comfort. There is also some great advice. For example, advising Connor not to lie because it "helps Lucifer". Regardless of whether or not you believe in Lucifer as an actual entity, or any type of negative "war lord", is of no consequence. The truth is that when you lie you hurt yourself. Lies are one of the quickest ways to lower your vibration and negatively affect your aura, and that can leave you open to the influence of lower energies, vibrations, and entities. This can become a downward spiraling negative cycle. We lie because we are afraid of the truth, but once we lie and get away with it we are plagued either by the fear that we will get caught for that lie in the future, or by guilt which is another low-vibrating emotion that first we create, then we allow to attach to us, and finally we allow to grow. Make no mistake, we carry these lies around with us and they will do damage. These children, many of them, have come to speak the truth and so they must be given the support not to lie and not to live in fear of truth. Fear will drag them down and lead them off course. Lies will bind them. Together they can debilitate anyone. So, while no child or adult will tell the truth every time, it is important that these children have confidence in the fact that they need not fear speaking the truth and that a lie is easily corrected by being honest and asking for forgiveness. Forgiveness releases everything and love heals.

The other part of this dream that I adore is the concept that we are surrounded by angels who are there to watch over and protect us. We are not alone. We should all take heart in this fact and remember that while angels (forces of Light, positive energies) can do an awful lot on their own, asking for their help and knowing that they are there and will come to our aid is important as well. However, giving angels our permission to help us is crucial in allowing them greater involvement in our lives as they are required to honor our free will, and therefore cannot effect changes without our blessing. While this is a comfort to everyone, it is especially important for psychic children who may be experiencing things which are frightening or challenging for them. They may feel alone in their experiences or they may feel isolated, especially as they begin the transition to making this world a bigger part of their reality and "disconnecting" from other realms. It is during this time of integration, as they are forced to focus more and more on the here and now, that they become aware that not everyone is experiencing what they are and they may become confused or frightened. This fear and conflict as they attempt to reconcile both realities may cause them to shut down their intuition. I found that this can often be the time where negative experiences occur more often because while the Light plays by the rules honoring the free will of the individual, the Dark does not, and is always looking for loopholes and weaknesses. It is therefore of the utmost importance that they know that they are loved, they are protected both on this side and on the other, and that they can call for help or companionship at any time and receive it.

As a postscript to this dream, Connor later told me that during this visit Jesus had taken him to places such as Egypt and Bethlehem to show him "how people had lived", and for him to observe the cruelty of human behavior such as slavery and war. He also insisted that he saw vehicles that ran on "love" instead of fuel. I found all this so interesting, but Connor would not explain much more to me at the time. When I began writing this book I asked Connor if he would allow me to place him into hypnosis so that we could revisit this experience and get a little more information. He kindly agreed to do this for me. Below is part of the transcript that was the result of our session in November 2007, eight years after his initial experience. I chose not to include all of the information as some of it was personal and related only directly to Connor.

CP: What's happening?

C: *Outside its just calm…dark. Inside my head…at first it's just pitch black. Then it gets a little lighter every minute that passes by. Lighter and lighter it goes 'til finally it's light.*

CP: What do you see?

C: *I see a figure walking towards me through the white light. It's the only shape there. He or she casts a shadow because right now I don't know… what…who he or she is. He comes up to me.*

CP: Who is he?

C: *Jesus. Brown hair - long to his shoulders. His eyes, warm, caring and comforting. His face – distinct. You would recognize him in a crowd of people. His body shape – thin. He is sort of tall. He has sandals on his feet because it was the style they wore when he was alive.*

CP: How do you feel around him?

C: *Happy. Safe. Love.*

CP: Why has he come to you? What does he want to tell you?

C: *He wants to show me stuff in Heaven. I get a sneak peek of when I die (smiles)...where I will be living when I die unless I decide to come back down here again.*

CP: Do you know why he wants to show you this? Why it is important?

C: *Uh-uh (no).*

CP: He doesn't tell you?

C: *No. As with all great questions, the answers come in good time...We disappear and reappear there (Heaven).*

CP: How does that happen?

C: *He puts his arm on my shoulder. And we slowly fade into nothing and we slowly appear in Heaven.*

CP: Ok. What's it like?

C: *There are big buildings - skyscrapers. It looks a lot like Earth but the buildings aren't made of stone. They have a certain feel about them that makes me know they are not stone.*

CP: What does he want to show you in Heaven?

C: *He wants to show me …nothing is bad there.*

CP: How do they keep bad things out I wonder?

C: *The will of God helps them protect Heaven from Hell.*

CP: He told you about angels that are everywhere, the Dream Police and the Sky Police. Can you explain what they do – these angels that are everywhere?

C: *The Sky Police patrol the sky for anything that might hurt us, or birds, or living things in any way. The Dream Police make sure that no bad dreams get into your head…or at least they try anyway. But not even angels are… even angels make mistakes.*

(Other questions and discussion here which are personal and not relative to others)

C: *God is mysterious and yet simple in some ways, and in others…it depends on your view, your beliefs, how you picture Him. Satan is absolutely easy to figure out. He is like an open book. That's the difference between them. Satan just wants destruction and war. God wants peace and love and for everyone to be safe but He knows that people die, and He allows it, and when their time comes He knows they will return to Earth because they love* it down there, and it's an interesting adventure for everyone until they die. And they tell God how it's doing, why…how people are so naïve sometimes. Satan infects people. He causes more bad, hate, war. Sometimes he even gets to them when they are still…when they are (very young).

CP: Why does he (Satan) want to do this do you think?

C: *Because he wants to turn…he wants to gain more power. Like all power-hungry maniacs.*

CP: How did you feel when you were up in Heaven?

C: *Joyful.*

CP: Did Jesus take you to other places? To show you how people had lived?

C: *He showed me **while** I was in Heaven.*

CP: How did that happen?

C: *They have a TV screen that allows you to see how people lived…how they live. He showed me Egypt, Rome, Greece, Europe, Mongolia, and finally China and Japan.*

CP: Did he show you present day or was it ancient, or a mix?

C: *Ancient up to present day to show me how much Earth has changed over the thousands of years.*

CP: Why was this important?

C: *Because Good is change. Evil is staying the same. He showed me how people were stupid, uneducated and barbaric. They were butchering people, taking their livestock and wealth, and daughters.*

CP: What did Jesus want you to learn from this?

C: *I think I know…that no matter how bad it may seem, there is always a little chance that humanity might get it right once in a while.*

CP: Why do you think that he wanted you, specifically, to understand this?

C: *I don't know and I don't want to question it.*

CP: O.K. He told you never to lie. Can you explain this to me?

C: *Because when you lie…it affects you and other people negatively. And it's because Satan feeds on negative energy and the more negative energy we put out the stronger he will become.*

(Connor indicates that he wants to come out of hypnosis and that he has shared all that he is willing to.)

CP: How did you get back into your room? Did Jesus bring you home?

C: *Yes. He brought me to this place where we were before, then he walked back and the light grew fainter and it became darker and darker still.*

CP: How did you feel when he left?

C: *Ok. Not as good as I felt in Heaven, but ok.*

I chose to include this because I think that the message is so clear. We have the choice and the ability to change for the better and to improve ourselves and our world. Even more than that, we have the responsibility to change, grow and improve, and we have all the support and love required to accomplish these tasks. All we need is the individual and collective will along with the belief that we can change the old patterns of thought and behavior. In my opinion, if we allow them to, these children can help us to accomplish just that.

Clouds & Multi-Colored Rain

Around December 5, 2001, Emmet saw what appeared to be a black door which hovered just below the ceiling in his room. He was frightened of the door not knowing what could come out of it as it was, as I was to learn later on, a portal. Strangely, he never questioned why or how the door came to be there. This black door remained there for approximately two weeks. I believe that at least part of the purpose of this door was to put Emmet in a place of fear and distract him. As I have said before, when a child, or anybody, sits in fear or is focused on something which causes them to be fearful their level of vibration drops, they are distracted and unable to accomplish the things they need to do, and they also become vulnerable.

Not being able to see this door myself, and being at a loss as to what to do about it I finally suggested that Emmet ask God or Jesus to help in getting rid of the door. On December 19th, the day he made his request, cloud-like objects appeared which emitted what Emmet described as multi-colored rain and the black doorway disappeared. The multi-colored rain followed Emmet around for quite a while afterwards. I believe these were angels, and they certainly had a positive effect on Emmet and his surroundings. So I can only assume that his request was heard and answered!

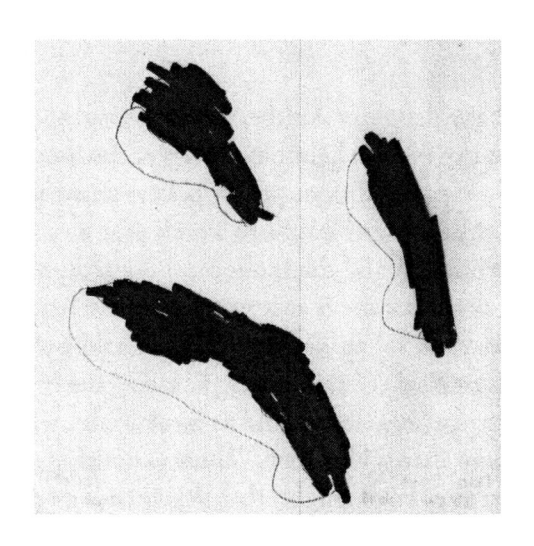

Clouds

To see this in color go to *www.aknowing.com* or to the Facebook page: A Knowing-Living with Psychic Children

Multi-colored Rain

To see this in color go to *www.aknowing.com* or to the Facebook page: A Knowing-Living with Psychic Children

Blue Light

In July 2002, my daughter Anithe, who was then age four, saw over a period of nights a sky-blue or light-blue entity at the foot of her bed. It is interesting that in some traditions people believe that the foot of the bed is where our Guardian Angel stands to watch over us at night. This entity's presence thrilled her and she spoke most excitedly about it. She was perplexed that I could not see it as it was so clear to her. So I explained that some people could see things that others could not and that it was wonderful that she could see this entity. She told me it was her angel. I include this picture because to me, and to most adults, what she drew appears to be no more than a blue blob. There is nothing to indicate to us, based on what we have been taught, that this is how an angel might look or present itself, but that is how this being appeared to her and this being was her angel. I can say this with conviction because Anithe "knew" it and I am in no position to question her belief or knowing of what this was.

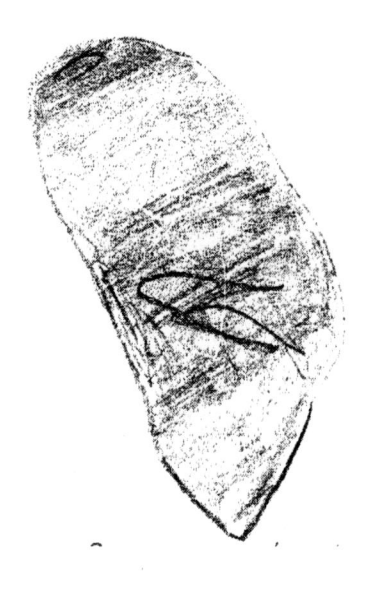

Anithe's Angel

To see this in color go to www.aknowing.com or to the Facebook page: A Knowing-Living with Psychic Children

These entities of Light are by us and around us all the time. Children can sense them and see them without effort or ceremony. I found it interesting that she depicted this angel in blue, a color I was to discover later on is the color of protection and is often associated with the Archangel Michael. Isn't it beautiful that they can see and know that they are protected and watched over? I cringe when I think about what might have happened had I scoffed at her description and illustration, or if I had told her that angels didn't appear like this. What if I had insisted that they had halos and wings and wore ancient-style clothing? Surely she would have felt conflicted and upset. And surely, the next time she saw this entity she would have either become confused and possibly scared by it or she may have chosen to ignore it. By ignoring it she would have closed down her ability to see angels and by becoming confused or conflicted between what she knew and felt was true and what I, her mother, had said she would have brought in self-doubt and may have invited fear around her instead of love and peace. So beware of what you say to children and remember that how they perceive and depict what they see may not match what we have been taught to expect.

Pink & Blue Light

From August 1, 2002, Emmet began to see a Light Being that was pink inside and was surrounded by blue light. The color pink is the color of unconditional love while blue is the color of protection. This entity was accompanied by a return of the multi-colored rain, which we now associated with the angelic realm. Emmet often saw this Light Being at night hovering at the foot of his bed and it brought Emmet comfort during the weeks it remained with him. I believe that this may have been one of his Guardian Angels - my children feel that a person can have many guardian angels, not just one, depending on many factors including need. Whatever it was, its presence brought him peace and joy.

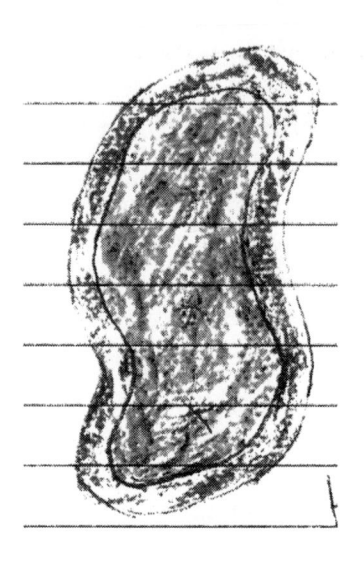

Emmet's Angel

To see this in color go to www.aknowing.com or to the Facebook page: A Knowing- Living with Psychic Children

At the time that this pink and blue entity arrived, we had just moved home and country and our living situation was not optimal. I believe that Emmet was experiencing stress and fear at the upheaval and felt uncomfortable where we were living. It was then that this beautiful entity arrived – when Emmet needed it most. As he was almost seven, and at the cusp of when many children's psychic abilities begin to fade, I was grateful that his had not and he was therefore able to recognize the help that was being sent to him. We benefit from any type of positive energy sent to us in all forms regardless of whether or not we can see them or sense them, but I find that having the conscious knowledge and being able to recognize that something is occurring in a more "tangible" way (through one of our five senses) increases its effect because it appeals directly to our problematic and fearful conscious mind while also positively affecting our subconscious, our auric fields, and our soul. It's sad that our society teaches children that these beautiful experiences and entities are not real (they are mythical beings that sprang from the attempts of ancients to explain their environment or are a product of imagination); are not valued (individuals will be doubted and ridiculed if they speak of these experiences); or accessible in any direct way (we teach them that in general children cannot interact with the Divine as apparently only "approved" prophets who were alive thousands of years ago, or people who are devoutly religious and therefore are associated with a sanctioning institution, have the ability to interact with the Divine and others from beyond the veil). Why deny these children? To what purpose? What do we, as individuals or as societies, gain from this approach? It is quite an absurd attitude and situation, and yet we accept it and perpetuate it to the detriment of our children and ourselves.

Six years later, when Emmet was going through a stressful time, he observed another entity by his bed that followed him around for a few hours. This entity was one of healing and protection and was made up of bands or rings of light. The colors it emitted were green at its center followed by violet, pink, blue and deep purple. It was quite large and put him at peace. His emotional state drastically improved following this visit and he was able to handle the situation that was causing him distress with ease.

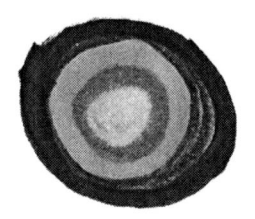

Entity By Emmet's Bed

To see this in color go to www.aknowing.com or to the Facebook page: A Knowing-

Living with Psychic Children

Voices Calling & Singing

Beginning on March 7, 2001 Emmet began to share with me that he could sometimes hear voices. These voices were pleasant and he described them as female and said that at times they sounded like my voice. Sometimes they were singing. Often he would answer them or call to them, but he found that they did not reply despite the fact that at times he actually heard them calling his name. He would hear them in the still of the night, at bedtime, when there was no other discernable sound and, therefore, he could not have been mistaking peripheral noise for these voices. Many times when all was quiet and I would be putting them to sleep he would suddenly shout out, "What?" It was at these times that he would share what was occurring with me. I am sure there were many other incidents that I was not aware of merely because he chose not to respond to the voices out loud. He was frustrated about his inability to find out what these voices wanted. He explained, *"The voices come from different places, but never answer me when I say 'What?"* I believe that these voices were angels, and while they did not respond to his queries and responses, it seems that their voices and songs acted as a protection and to lift up his spirit and level of vibration. I also feel that it served to remind and reassure him that he was never alone and that "they" had not forgotten about him.

Angel of the Six Hearts

On May 28, 2003 Emmet spoke of an angel that he had seen. He described this angel as being one that *"Resembles the Wings of Six Hearts,"* and said that, *"He had a light so bright that I could not even open my eyes."* The angel held a shield that he threw to Emmet- again a symbol of protection.

Angel that resembles the Wings of Six Hearts

To see a clearer copy go to www.aknowing.com or to the Facebook page: A Knowing-Living with Psychic Children

The picture of this angel, if nothing else, communicates tremendous power and intention of purpose. He is depicted with three sets of wings, a concept that Emmet would not have been exposed to at that time. Emmet did not provide this angel's name as he did not seem to think a specific name was necessary or important, but my friend John Collins believes it to be the Archangel Gabriel despite it having three sets of wings which are normally attributed to the Seraphim.

I want to draw attention to the necklace that this angel is wearing. I was amazed by the fact that Emmet had included it because three years earlier he had made a necklace out of paper like this for me claiming that it would catch God's voice and put it into my heart if I wore it. He had not been shown that necklace since he had given it to me and so this makes its appearance around the neck of this obviously powerful angelic being all the more remarkable and mystifying. This necklace is discussed in Chapter 4: Mystical Communications & Dreams.

Jesus: The Angel You Are

This is one of my favorites because of its beauty and its significance to Emmet. In September 2004, Emmet shared an experience that had occurred a few weeks earlier while we were on vacation in Kerry in Ireland. In his description Emmet told me of being surrounded by white and gold light, which at the time meant nothing to me. It was not until many years later as I studied to become a Reiki Master that I learned that gold light is referred to as Christ Light. I mention this because it is so easy to put these important and valid statements down to imagination or wishful thinking…but they are not and often the validity can be found within the detail. So even if your child is saying things that you cannot accept as true or do not understand, keep a log. When you begin to grow and learn, you can refer back to these incidents, as I did, and watch as information and truths that you overlooked or discounted before leap off the page at you. Prepare to be humbled, amazed and touched for as interesting as it may be to read about someone else's child, nothing can surpass the impact of it coming from your own.

Emmet's picture and description are below:

Jesus' Visit: The Angel You Are

To see a clearer copy go to www.aknowing.com or to the Facebook page: A Knowing-Living with Psychic Children

"One night Jesus came to me. He put his hands together like this (like a child praying) and I was lifted out of bed and surrounded by gold and white light, and he said, 'Now to show you the angel you are.'" -E

He never told me what Jesus showed him about himself, and I never asked as it is not for me to know. I assume it is that Emmet, like all of us, is Divine and his essence is the Light of the Divine. If only we could all remember this more often and incorporate it in a more real and active way into our daily lives.

The timing of this experience has always mystified me to some degree but I suppose, for whatever reason, Emmet needed to be reminded at that moment of who he really was and it was around this time that Emmet's psychic gift appeared to begin to retreat or rather morph into a more "practical" type of psychic ability. He went from actively knowing, seeing, hearing and smelling things to having incredible insight into our world and how things work. Perhaps, knowing that Emmet was about to close down large parts of his abilities Jesus, or whoever makes these decisions on the other side, felt that it was important to remind him one last time of who he is, what he can achieve, and how much love and support there is for him – as indeed there is for all of us. As I mentioned in Chapter 1, Emmet later explained to me,

"It's not that I don't want my gifts, I am just taking a break right now. I just want to be normal and do fun things. I'll get back to them when I am ready."

Sometimes I envy these children and their interactions with Beings of Light, but I always also reflect on the reverse side of the coin and recognize that I would probably not be able to handle the other things that they see and experience from the darker areas of existence. There is also a lot of responsibility that goes along with having this type of ability that many of us would not want to accept. So I try to admire but not covet.

These are only a few examples of the direct interaction and communication that children have with the Divine and it is so beautiful. I hope this chapter has given people heart and hope and will remind us all that we are watched, protected, guided, prompted, and most importantly, loved.

Chapter 3
Alien Encounters

Alien encounters can accompany psychic activity – sometimes but not always – and occasionally the lines between the two types of experiences can be blurred. My children had three tangible experiences of which I am aware and which I have decided to include because it is important that no experience is discounted or considered invalid. Alien encounters can be more elusive to track or analyze because those who experience them are often asleep at the time when the encounter initiates and there appears to be a desire or a concerted effort by alien beings to ensure that people do not remember. This does seem to contrast sharply with what is considered to be purely spiritual experiences, where at least part of the purpose of the experience is that we remember as much as possible with clarity, and that we carry that experience and any messages we may have received with us.

I mentioned before that our society does not promote or support psychic phenomena and that those with psychic ability are often portrayed as "kooks", although thankfully this attitude and perception is changing. This is even truer of the alien and UFO phenomenon, and those who have been brave enough to come forward are often ridiculed and maligned. Most of these people have had nothing to gain by sharing their experiences and often request anonymity as they fear derision and abuse. What we, as a culture and a society, are so fearful of, so threatened by in relation to alien and UFO experiences, I do not know. But it is there. Many other cultures are open and accepting of these stories while there are governments that openly report and discuss incidents which they have been made aware of or involved with and still cannot explain. In fact, just recently the French and British Governments have opened their files regarding reports and their investigations related to UFO activity. The Mexicans, Russians, and Nordic countries seem to report UFO incidents without derision or multiple layers of mystery. So why are we, the United States of America, who are usually the leaders in cutting-edge thinking and who pride ourselves in being open-minded, so far behind when it comes to our attitudes and disclosure in this area?

I have read many theories and ideas as to why our government will not "come clean" in this regard, and I have come to the conclusion that we may never know what the rationale or thought process has been over the years. It may have begun for a good and honest reason, and might have been meant to be a temporary situation. But secrets and lies grow exponentially and there is power and money involved with information and knowledge so there has never really been an impetus for anyone or any group to operate in a different and open way. It would also seem that over the years as people vied for power, responsibilities, knowledge, and controls were split and subdivided to such as degree that by now, I would guess, even those involved at quite a high level probably don't know what the real and complete truth is. I am thankful that I no longer feel the need to have anyone validate the fact that this activity is occurring now *as it has throughout human history*, but it would be the responsible and honorable thing for all governments to come forward and offer full disclosure and support, especially for those who have been traumatized or haunted by their experiences. I greatly admire those individuals who are working to attain this and feel strongly that we should continually strive for facts and truth and insist on accountability from our institutions and governments. However, in the end, whether or not our government or other governments choose to disclose UFO and ET information, it does not change the reality that people are seeing things that cannot be explained away as swamp gas, illuminated duck bottoms, or weather balloons and they are experiencing things that are not the result of eating too much pizza late at night or due to the fact that they watched a Science Fiction movie or two. The fact of the matter is that these experiences happen, and for the most part those who experience them are not mentally unstable. More and more people who are in respected positions are coming forward to share what they have experienced both in their personal lives and within a work capacity, as is illustrated through Steven Greer's "Disclosure Project" and James Fox's "I Know What I Saw" documentary. So look to these people and projects if you require confirmation of this phenomenon and not to the United States Government.

Children who share ET and UFO experiences should be taken seriously and their stories should be handled gently and with respect. Most are unaware that speaking of alien encounters or UFOs is a cause for fear, aggressive disbelief, derisive hilarity, or a frantic visit the psychiatrist, and if they are aware of this potential then a child who shares this type of information is showing great bravery and trust by taking a risk by exposing themselves in this manner. So should your child speak of such an experience, do not panic or laugh and definitely do not deny or dismiss their revelation. Approach them from a centered and calm position to insure that they do not pick up any extremes in emotion from you and despite what you may be thinking or feeling attempt to deal with it as if it is a very ordinary and every day event. Try to engage them and in the process do your best to determine how they feel about what they saw or experienced, as this is really what is most important. Always remember that in this situation the most reliable source is your child as they are the one who experienced the event. As words can be limiting, especially for younger children, ask them to draw a picture of their encounter. Often the real emotion of the child and the personalities of the entities will come through in their art. It also helps them to remember and communicate minute details that are often lost during verbal discussion. If possible, watch the child as they are drawing. Take note of their facial expressions as they illustrate their experience, but don't interrupt them with questions as that may break the flow from their subconscious – save your questions for when they are done. Look at the colors they use, and how they approach the figures they are drawing. Are the smiling and using the pencil normally, or are they furrow-browed and moving the pencil in a hard and aggressive manner? As you discuss the experience you may want to casually ask them if the encounter they are sharing was their first – often it isn't, it is merely the first time they have felt inclined to share.

It is difficult to advise anyone about how to feel or what to do in these cases. Again, I can only emphasize that you listen to the child. Were they happy, excited, or frightened? Do they consider the alien(s) to be friendly, fun, grumpy or scary? Did the alien entity or entities do or say anything that your child feels was threatening or was the atmosphere a positive one that your child participated in freely and enjoyed? The probability is that they will express joy about most encounters and beings as it is often the emotion of fear that clouds the experience as negative, and fear in relation to these experiences and entities usually do not take hold until much later in life. No matter what your child describes or how you feel about the incident and the aliens involved, it is important to keep the lines of communication open with your child regarding this and any future incidents that they may experience, so remain emotionally steady and approachable.

The only recommendation I can make should a parent feel that the contact has a more underhanded agenda is to consider having the child initiated into Reiki I as this will alter and elevate the rate at which their energy vibrates. This is not guaranteed to work, but it can have an effect. Being initiated into Reiki will elevate and change the child's vibrational level and can prevent negative incidents from reoccurring. It will not harm the child in any way. Again, I stress that this is not a guarantee, but personal experience has shown me that doing this does seem to result in blocking or providing protection against many different kinds of non-third dimensional unpleasant encounters. I know that some people recommend telling these entities that their activity is counter to our freedom of choice, but I do not know of any proof that this makes any difference, nor do I feel that it is rational to expect a child to do this in any circumstance, let alone during one as unusual as an alien encounter.

As to the experiences that my children have shared with me, thus far they have been all positive ones involving benevolent beings. They have caused them no fear or trepidation as you will see from the following examples. If anything, my children feel a great amount of affection and joy in relation to the beings they have interacted with. I feel that each of the experiences falls into a different descriptive category – Out-of-Body, Dream, and Physical experiences – although people may disagree with my assessment and categorizations.

"Jesus" & the Flying Machine: Out-of-Body Experience

On October 19, 2001 Emmet described an incident that had occurred at an earlier date, although I have no idea when it occurred as he was too young to really understand the concept of time. I have no doubt, from the way Emmet described what had happened and the detail he provided when describing and illustrating the craft, that he did have this experience. From what I can gather, this was not a physical experience, but involved his energy body entering the craft.

He described lying in bed and there being a bright light. He said that he floated out of the window and up towards the craft, which he found amazing and fun. Emmet said he had been taken by "Jesus" in a flying machine that "Jesus" had made himself. The craft had been constructed for the purpose of taking pictures of "bad people" to show God so that God could understand what people are doing. There were many glowing lights outside of the craft. Inside the craft Emmet sat in a seat directly behind "Jesus". He had to wear a mask to breathe which Emmet said had a vine coming out of it which led to a box. Jesus also had a vine that connected into his belt. They hovered over the Earth. "Jesus" showed him many things but Emmet was not able to remember them. He returned to his bed in the same way as he had entered the craft.

He went on to draw the craft, the design of which is below. According to Emmet, within the craft he saw three areas/things that were marked and that he remembered specifically. There was an area marked F which he described as the "fire" that made the craft move (engine/propulsion system); an area marked L that he said meant love and that provided protection; and a box marked U that provided air.

Outside of craft

To see a clearer copy go to www.aknowing.com or to the Facebook page: A Knowing- Living with Psychic Children

Inside of craft

To see a clearer copy go to www.aknowing.com or to the Facebook page: A Knowing- Living with Psychic Children

I found this incident very difficult to handle for two reasons (beyond the fact that I was upset at the idea of anyone coming in to our house uninvited and interacting with one of my children without my knowledge or permission). The first was that at the time I did not give much weight to the whole UFO and alien abduction/contact scenario. The second reason was that this entity claimed to be Jesus, which obviously was not true. So either this entity was misleading Emmet in order to get Emmet to trust and follow him, or what the alien was actually attempting to communicate was that he was a "friend" or a good guy who meant no harm and that it was safe for Emmet to enter the craft. Was it a lie by an intelligent being that had ulterior motives or just a misunderstanding of a very young child? I didn't know then and I still have no concrete answer. In the end I looked to Emmet's emotional and physical expressions for clues and cues and realized that he clearly was not upset or concerned about the experience and actually seemed to have enjoyed the interaction. He had felt safe and at peace with the entity, whoever he may have been, and so I knew that I should put aside my own fears and be at peace with it as well.

It can take time to put these good thoughts into practice so do not put yourself under any undue pressure. After this discussion with Emmet, it took many years of research and growth on my part before I was able to accept the fact that these incidents had occurred and that they were not something that should cause doubt, panic, or embarrassment. I was torn because on the one hand, as his mother, I knew beyond a shadow of a doubt that he was telling me the truth about something that really had happened, but my "rational" and pre-conditioned prejudices would not allow me to accept it fully. I knew that he held no fear towards this being or the experience, but I had been conditioned to fear in order to protect. It was a struggle, but it is a struggle I don't regret because it forced me to open books and talk to wonderful people and learn and grow so much... but it wasn't easy. So do not feel that just because your child shares an alien or psychic encounter with you that, as their parent, it should be an easy thing to accept. It isn't always and that is part of the challenge - to open our minds and to grow. If we were already "there" we would not need the nudge, or in some cases the "body slam", that these children are here to provide us with. Waking up can be hard when you have slept for so long!!

The Reptilian & the Telescope: Dream Experience

Immediately upon waking on the morning of September 10, 2006 Emmet told me of dream he had had. While I believe this was more dream and less alien experience, I include it here as it is alien related and does have significance. Sometimes an alien-related story is a physical experience, some are energy-body or out-of-body experiences, while other times they are dreams and each one is equally valuable. While this dream was Emmet's, I think that its message and significance applies to us all. The dream is described below:

Emmet was in a place where there was a huge telescope that was plugged into a computer of some sort. He was looking through the telescope at the Universe. In the room where he was he noticed a brown book with gold writing. A bird, which he described as a chicken, was standing on the book and was blinking constantly. Emmet looked at the chicken for a moment and then returned his attention to the telescope. This time he noticed a huge shadow. He moved the telescope towards the shadow and saw that it was being cast by a Reptilian-type alien who had large feathery things on his head. Emmet claimed that the Reptilian was very nice.

After much discussion with Emmet and a good bit of research, I believe I can interpret and explain its significance. In this dream, the telescope plugged into the computer represents the ability to acquire/discover, process, and retain knowledge and wisdom. The book with the golden writing relates to his purpose or mission. We all come here with a purpose to complete certain tasks and missions and we need to discover what they are. The blinking chicken represents doubt and lack of courage – doubt about ourselves and what we believe. Doubt about who we really are. We have to open our eyes and our hearts and have the courage to see our beauty and power in order to erase the only thing that stands in the way of us accomplishing our mission - self-doubt. The nice reptilian with the feathers represents a higher power/force or the coming together of consciousness (feathers) with physical reality (reptilian/serpent). So the reptilian represents both us, as human beings, **and** that which created us and the Universe that we inhabit. And as we are all one (or interconnected and interrelated), and as we are destined to rejoin our Source, the Reptilian representation in Emmet's dream makes a lot of sense as it represents us individually and as a collective. So to recap the significance of the dream: he incarnated/we incarnate as humans on Earth in order to rise to the challenge of understanding who we really are and completing the task of understanding that there is no separation and that we are all one. We come to learn to behave in a manner that reflects the ultimate truth of our origin, and so we must learn to love ourselves and one another so that we may then ascend and "rejoin" the Source from which we are never truly separated. (It is a really more of a process of awakening than rejoining as the separation is an illusion.) We have been given all of the tools required to accomplish this, we merely need to open our eyes and our hearts in order to achieve it. Well, that is my interpretation at any rate.

Now I realize that there are many frightening tales regarding the reptilian alien race but keep in mind that this was a dream experience and not a physical experience and so would have been very symbolic. Emmet described this entity as being "nice" and, as I stated before, it is that child's opinion and assessment of situations and characters that is the most important factor of all when looking at these incidents. Finally, we are not aware of every race or every off-shoot of each race within the Universe and I would assume that, like human beings, not every individual of every race is guaranteed to behave in exactly the same manner. It may also be that there have been reptilian races that have been kindly towards humanity and have worked with us to educate us such as Quetzalcoatl is said to have done. But as it was a dream experience, I chose to analyze it from a symbolic prospective. I hope I have done it justice.

Red & Grey Aliens: Physical Experience

In 2005, Anithe, then age seven, told me of an incident that involved aliens in the room she shared with her brothers. She insisted that it had actually occurred and was not a dream. On that particular evening she had fallen asleep in the same bed as Emmet and I had decided to leave her there rather than risk disturbing her by moving her into her own bed. The following is the description of what she explained occurred on that night:

Anithe awoke to find there were many aliens in the room. Emmet awoke beside her. The small and medium sized aliens were either grey or greenish-grey. They were moving in a pattern around a large alien who was very tall and very thin. This alien was red and had what she described as stars or lights moving around under its skin – its arms were extendable to quite a distance. She felt no fear and insisted that they were all "nice" but that the tallest one was the nicest of all. The red alien reached out and gently took her teddy bear. It seemed confused and interested in it (Anithe said that she felt that it was perplexed by it, perhaps trying to understand its purpose or function). After a few minutes, Emmet asked the red alien to return Anithe's teddy bear to her, as it was important to Anithe. The red alien immediately complied.

Red & Grey Aliens

To see this in color go to www.aknowing.com or to the Facebook page: A Knowing-Living with Psychic Children

I absolutely loved this story as it was so full of gentle wonder. Unlike the other two experiences discussed in this chapter, these aliens actually were there and did interact with Anithe and Emmet in a physical state. Emmet also has a memory of this experience, specifically of when he asked for the teddy bear back, but not much else about this event stuck in his memory. I believe this is partly because this visit was specifically related to Anithe. It seems that these beings came to see and interact with her, but did not make any attempt to prevent Emmet from being involved. It was a beautiful interchange.

Three years later, in order to glean more information regarding this experience, I asked Anithe if we could use hypnosis together so that I might ask her a few questions. During the session I contacted her Higher Self in order to question it about the meeting and its purpose. Remember that while I was speaking to her Higher Self, it can be somewhat limited by the language skills of Anithe who was ten at the time. The following transcript begins after her Higher Self had been engaged. Anithe is referred to here in the third person.

C: She (Anithe) told me that she was visited one night by a very tall red alien with lights under its skin…and he was accompanied by some small grey aliens. Do you know what I am speaking of?

A: Yes, I do.

C: Why did they come to see her?

A: *At that time she was doubting a bit…she was doubting aliens existed so they wanted to come down to be sure that she didn't stop believing.*

C: Is it important to them that she believe in them?

A: *It's very important to them that she believes.*

C: Why is that?

A: *She is very powerful and she will be able to help them if they got in trouble.*

C: She would be able to help the aliens?

A: *Yes…even if it wasn't physically.*

C: What do you mean by that? (No response). But you said she was important to them? Is that right?

A: Her belief in them is important because without the belief she wouldn't be able to help them. If she needed to, that is. She works on an energy level. She can help them on that level – an energy level if they need it… so they need her to believe in them. Anithe is a very powerful being and has energy and healing powers that are on an incredible level.

C: So she is this incredible being…so is part of her job to help this red race and other races…or just the one race?

A: She can help pretty much any race but…even though she can't do it physically she can do it in an energy sort of way.

C: Can she decide to do this type of work on a conscious level or does it always have to happen in the background?

A: Well, she can send out energy consciously but it is hard.

C: Can Anithe ever call on these aliens if she ever needs them?

A: Yes, she can but it would be hard for them to come physically so they would come in her dream.

C: This red race…besides wanting to be sure Anithe continued to believe in them…was there any other reason why they came to see her?

A: Well, they were particularly interested in how Anithe worked and how she thought.

C: Ok. Did they take her from the house or did they just come to visit her in her room?

A: They came to visit only. They did not take her from her room.

C: How did they get here…how did they come during this visit?

A: They went through a portal, but it was invisible so it's like they just appeared. They did it that way so they (Anithe and her brother) would think it was a dream and it would not frighten them.

C: How about the little greys? What were they doing there? What was their purpose?

A: They were helping the red alien travel.

C: So that was their job? To help with travel?

A: Yes.

C: The very tall alien seemed so extraordinary. Can you tell me about this "red" race?

A: The red race is a group of aliens, who don't really stay in one place… they move around like nomads. They are very kind and always try to help. They wouldn't do anything bad.

C: Yes, she said she felt very safe with them and that the (red) alien was very interested in her teddy bear. Why is that?

A: It's because he wasn't really familiar with how they…how much energy was coming out of this lifeless toy.

C: Energy?

A: Yes, energy that she had put into the bear herself. The red alien was not familiar with this.

C: So you mean, Anithe had put energy into her bear by holding it and things like that?

A: Yes.

C: And then the red alien was able to pick up on the energy that was stored in the bear and was interested in the bear because of this?

A: Yes.

C: Ok. Why are they interested in the Earth?

A: *It's because the Earth is so different to where they have been. And the people in it (humans) are so different from what they have seen and how they have loads of different languages within the same group and they (the red aliens) all speak the same (language). Also, it makes them wonder why, if humans are so nice, and everyone that lives on Earth is so nice, why they wouldn't want to live together (in peace).*

C: So the red race…part of the reason they are interested in us is because unlike them we have many different languages…and beliefs. But their race …do they all speak the same language and have the same beliefs?

A: Yes.

C: Why do different races of aliens come to this earth?

A: *Some come to see what the earth looks like and others come to leave hints to tell humans that they are there.*

C: So they want us to know that they are here?

A: Yes.

C: Why is that important?

A: *Because they don't believe that the humans are evil and they don't want the humans to believe that they are evil.*

Now I am sure people reading this would have wished me to push for more information, and I would have loved to but I had to exercise restraint because it takes a while to get someone to the depths of relaxation and detachment that is required in order to contact the Higher Self, and I did not want to keep Anithe in that state for too long as she was so young and it can be tiring and a bit disorienting.

I do hope that the information I was able to gather provides some insight and some hope to those whose children have had similar experiences. Understand that you and your children are not alone in that others are having these experiences. Also keep in mind that even the smallest of us have Higher Selves who are a part of us and who direct us as well as Higher Beings who work with us and watch over us as much as we allow them to.

Chapter 4

Mystical Communications & Dreams

Children are very open to mystical communications and activity. When I say this I mean that they can spontaneously remember past lives or parts of past lives; they can communicate with all manner of beings that exist at higher and lower levels of vibration and in different dimensions; they can access glimpses of deeper truths and future events; and they have dreams of significance. They can do all this and more, and they can do it without effort, ceremony, or conscious intent. Children, because they have not been fully conditioned to block things out that are of other dimensions, have access to and possess a knowing which is precious and invaluable to us as individuals and as a collective group. It can be hard at times to differentiate between these different types of experiences and to determine how to categorize or deal with them. Some are glaringly obvious, especially as the child grows older and develops a better grasp of language which improves communication, while some experiences seem to defy categorization. Unfortunately, as children grow and become more focused on the here and now, their ability to communicate may improve but their connection and openness to anything beyond the third dimension often lessons and in particular their memories of past lives fade as they give in more and more to the life they are currently experiencing. So what is gained on the one hand is often lost on the other. I cannot say for sure that my analysis of every communication in this section is accurate, but I have done my best based on years of experience, research, and discussions with my children.

What I had more difficulty with was getting my children to explain **how** they came to know things except for when the vehicle of communication had been glaringly obvious. In other words, were they born with this knowing/understanding, did it come to them in a dream, did an entity appear and explain things to them, did they hear a voice, or were they suddenly filled with a need to share something that had just entered their consciousness? Most of the time my children found my interest and questions regarding the vehicle of communication to be perplexing and superfluous as they could not conceive of the need to understand **how** the information or statement had been communicated to them - it just had. I realize, of course, that my children are right and that understanding the process is not as important as recognizing and understanding the message, and much time, thought, and energy can be wasted attempting to figure this out. This disparity in approach illustrates the difference between adults and children – children trust and accept (open channels) while adults question and analyze (closed or blocked communication). So don't waste too much time trying to figure out "how" your child came to know something, just understand that the Universe is flexible and it will alter the modes of contact and communication as required in order to reach out and touch us.

What most adults fail to realize is that we too experience otherworldly communication and guidance that we are often not fully cognizant of and that, if questioned, we would not be able to describe "how" it had occurred. It takes many forms and it occurs quite often, we just tend to ignore it. As I said before, the difference between most adults and young children is that children listen and accept, while we doubt and ignore. Well, I know that I do. I have often asked for an answer or for guidance only to receive it and then either miss it or overlook the response entirely until years later because it did not come in the form I expected; I deny the fact that I received an answer when it is not the response I wanted; or I absolutely fail to understand even the most obvious response to my requests for various reasons including the fact that I am too literal and have a tendency to question and doubt everything. Children are not like this. Because they do not perceive division or barriers between dimensions, all interaction is fluid and is "normal" to them. They do not yet have pre-conditioned ideas of a limited and structured reality or restrictive and exclusive boundaries that dictate that certain experiences and communications are not possible. These are ideas and concepts that are erected and reinforced by society and religious beliefs. And as they do not question the existence of the Source, the mode of the communication or interaction, or the truth of the message, they are open receivers.

God's Secret

On March 16, 2000 as we were driving to school to collect my eldest son, Emmet was repeating the line, *"Heard me"* over and over. After we pulled into the parking lot I asked him about this statement, which I found perplexing. The following conversation ensued. At the time Emmet was four years old.

"What are you saying Emmet?" -CP

"Heard me." -E

"What does that mean, 'heard me'?" -CP

"It means heard me…listen to me." -E

"Listen to who? To you?" -CP

He gazed out of the window unwilling to answer me.

"Emmet. I want to thank you for sharing your secret with me. Do you know what I am talking about?" -CP

"Yes, God's Secret." -E

"That's right." -CP

"When the people come, I will tell them the secret too." -E

"What people?" -CP

"God's people." -E

"Do you think that is your job…to tell God's people the secret?" -CP

"Yes, when they come." -E

On March 24th when attempting to clarify what he had meant by what he said in the car Emmet explained, *"I can only tell them if they know. If they don't know, I won't tell them."*

Now before anyone gets excited about this "secret", I should emphasize that Emmet never shared the specifics of this secret was with me and he has no idea now of what it could be. When I thanked him for sharing his secret, I was referring to his "last time secret" with Jesus. I never pushed his reference to "God's secret" as I believe it to one and the same thing. Based on the discussion that he and I had on March 24th I lean towards placing this episode in a Past-Life category and believe that this may have been a memory left over from when he was living a life as a Gnostic. The Gnostics were "people who knew", and the word Gnostic itself means knowledge, as they believed that they were the keepers of ancient and sacred wisdom and knowledge and that this knowledge would bring them salvation. The fact that they did not share their knowledge with others who were not Gnostics I feel relates directly to Emmet's statement on the 24th. What he was saying is that unless someone was a Gnostic and appropriately vetted and initiated, he would not, and indeed could not, share God's Secret(s) with them.

The Scrolls

I refer to these communications as "scrolls" because after Emmet wrote them he rolled them up in a manner that is consistent with a scroll. Also, he wrote them from right to left. These really are two of my favorite communications that came through Emmet. The first, which was a prayer, was initially delivered by him in what sounded like a different language. He related the scroll in this "language" while standing with his arms apart and his palms turned outwards. He brought his hands together in front of his chest and bowed after speaking each line. He would then translate what the meaning was in English so that I could understand him. I have no way of knowing now if it was indeed another language, and my guess would be that it was not. But what was clear is that he was imitating the sound of the language that he had heard the scroll delivered in and his delivery was consistent in its sound but also altered with each "word" without ever bringing in sounds that would seem inconsistent with the sounds he had made previously. He was able to repeat it consistently on several occasions on that day, but refused to repeat the prayer after that. Unfortunately, this scroll was lost soon after, but luckily I had the translation written down. The first scroll was written and handed to me on May 31, 2000.

"Earth: The world all around you. All around the world.

Animals: The animals all around you.

God & Jesus: God and Jesus are here. I always pray to you. I always love you."

When I asked him how he knew to write this information, he said quite seriously and with great reverence, *"God told me. I wrote them because I know that God is the greatest…Mommy, if you were me, you would write them too."* How can you argue with that?

The next set of scrolls was written in the summer of 2000. I include copies of these here not because I believe they are in any real written language but because the message is so potent. As I stated in Chapter 1, it is not what the drawing or writing mean to us that is important. What is significant is what the child states that they are. Like the first scroll, they were written from right to left and stated, "God Made Jesus", "For God and Jesus, Life is Them", and "For Nature, God is life".

God Made Jesus

To see this in color go to <u>www.aknowing.com</u> or to the Facebook page: A Knowing-Living with Psychic Children

For God and Jesus, Life is Them

To see this in color go to <u>www.aknowing.com</u> or to the Facebook page: A Knowing-Living with Psychic Children

For Nature, God is Life

To see this in color go to www.aknowing.com or to the Facebook page: A Knowing-

Living with Psychic Children

After leaving me speechless with these in my hand, he ran off to play with his siblings as if what he had shared with me was of no great significance, and this is a point I want to emphasize. Just because we feel that something mind-blowing has come through our child, we should not expect them to respond in the same way. What they are sharing is not news to them, nor are most of these communications meant for them. They already know within them what God is, what love is, and that they are not alone. They have a deep and inner understanding that does not require words, categorization, definition and analysis. More often than not, they are acting as messengers and teachers for us, for we are the ones that are blind and deaf groping around in the darkness and tripping ourselves up with our self-importance and our lack of "knowing". So they deliver these messages to wake us up, shake us up and open our hearts to the beauty and the life, both visible and invisible, that is all around us. They have come to hold our hands and lead us towards awareness.

I want to mention again that despite the fact that we did not practice any religion or speak of it at the time, we were a Christian household. My husband had been raised a Catholic while I had been brought up as a Protestant. I believe this is why Emmet used Christian symbols and references. The most important aspect of these scrolls is not the overtly Christian reference to Jesus, but the message behind them. Indeed, the fundamental point is that we are of God, we are One, eternally tied to our Maker and therefore to each other. Nature herself is our sister and we should treat her with the same love and respect as we wish to be treated ourselves. When we harm others or nature, we harm ourselves. There is no them and us, no here and there - everything and everyone is linked as everything has been brought into existence from the same Source. We must try to remember that everything that exists, all that there is, are just different aspects, expressions, and manifestations of God or the Source.

The Church Prayer

This is actually a necklace that Emmet made out of paper for me in November 2000 that he wanted me to wear. I was so worried about ruining it that I placed it into my ever-growing file and stupidly never wore it. I say stupidly, because it was made for me and I now understand that Emmet knew that I needed it and that it would have helped me. However, being completely out-of-touch and concerned with the wrong things (the preservation of the item as opposed to its beneficial effect), I didn't realize that I was meant to wear the amulet. Emmet called it "the church prayer" and when he gave it to me he explained, "*This catches God's voice and puts it in your heart so (that) you can hear what He is saying.*"

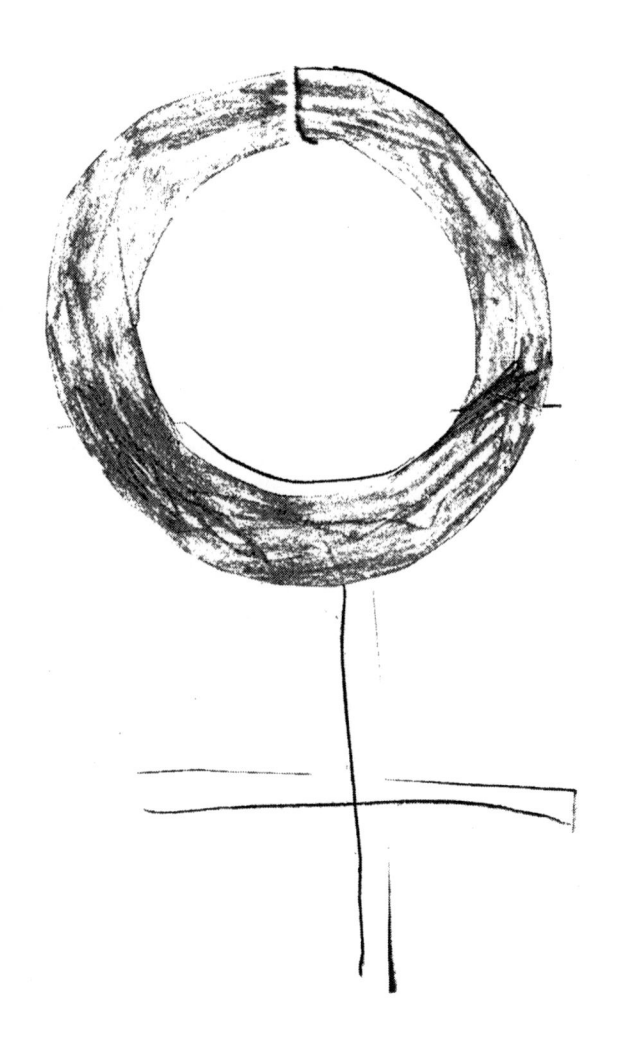

The Church Prayer

To see this in color go to www.aknowing.com or to the Facebook page: A Knowing-Living with Psychic Children

There are similar symbols in use today, notably the Sovereign's Orb that is held by the British monarch during their coronation. In this case, the cross stands above the orb and represents the responsibility of the monarch as the leader of the Church. It was also a Christian symbol of authority used throughout the Middle Ages in iconography, on coins, and as a part of royal regalia symbolizing God's dominion over the world. Many years later, in 2003, I discovered that in addition to being the symbol for Venus, copper, and God's dominion over the Earth, it is an alchemenical sigil that denotes the complete universal character of light and dark working together. It represents the chain of God coming into being. It symbolizes Cosmos as opposed to Chaos.

I find it amazing that such a young child in a completely secular environment could come up with such a symbol, let alone accurately link it to the concept of God bringing order and peace to my inner chaos and confusion, or even that he somehow "knew" that I needed to "hear" God's voice in order to sort out all the silent and unspoken confusion, fear, and questions that were whirling around within me.

The Garden

Drawn in the Fall of 2000, this picture and a portion of its description reminded me of the Garden of Eden. None of the children, however, had been exposed to the story at the time Emmet made this. The picture as explained by Emmet is of "God, the Moon, an eagle, a bat, and a happy house". Emmet explained, *"Under the rocks there is a beautiful garden. The rocks are there so people can't get in and steal and ruin the grass and flowers and apples and things."*

God, the Moon, an eagle, a bat and a happy house

To see a clearer copy go to <u>www.aknowing.com</u> or to the Facebook page: A Knowing-Living with Psychic Children

This picture is extremely symbolic, and therefore could easily be overlooked. As represented here, God is male energy while the Moon represents female energy. The eagle stands for the Truth or the Light. The bat represents intuition and the ability to see through the illusion of this "reality" we are experiencing that separates us from the Truth/Light in the same way that a bat can see through the dark. It may also represent communication and, therefore, may refer to prayer and the voice or thought-energy that travels between us and God. The Happy House is that which houses the soul – it is representative of our bodies where our souls take up residence for a short time. The rocks represent protection – that which protect our souls and will never allow the experiences we have while incarnated here on Earth to negatively affect or destroy that part of us, that brilliant spark, that is God. The garden signifies perfection - a place where nothing is sullied or tarnished, and it is a part of all of us and is always attainable.

Good & Evil

On May 28, 2003 Emmet shared the feeling that he had a role to play in this world but that he was unsure as to what it was. There was a great sense of frustration on his part that he did not know what this "something" was, but I suppose that is part of the challenge for all of us – to discover our roles and our missions and to find our way.

"I think that there is a fight…a big fight going on between good and evil, and somehow I am involved, but I don't know why." -E

Many children are coming into this world with a huge sense of purpose. The frustration for them is that most of them do not know what it is. They do not realize that just their mere presence here on Earth is helping to clear negativity, alter and raise the vibrations and consciousness of others and of the space around them, and this all contributes to positive change. Therefore they are not necessarily required to do anything specific to effect change and to fulfill their purpose except to maintain their high or unique level of vibration which, in and of itself, is a difficult challenge. So there is no need to agonize over career paths because no matter what vocation they choose they will help open the way for positive change to be introduced if we allow and accept it.

In term of children maintaining their vibrational level, this can be difficult as I have stated before. One thing that can challenge a child is when they feel psychically threatened, and this feeling is real. The threat comes from the lower energies and entities that have had so much influence over us and our world throughout known history. This influence and desire for power and control has not abated over time and continues to gain momentum and grow as we perpetuate the cycle of the machine that we helped to create and set in motion. They want more, not less, of the pie and they do not intend to go quietly, which should not be surprising. We only have to look at ourselves, at the human race, to understand the allure that drives and fuels the hungry determination for power and control. Most human beings will not relinquish power or control of their own volition, so you can imagine the fight that these entities and energies are willing to put up. We are all involved in this struggle, both internally and externally. However these children represent a particular threat to lower vibrating energies and entities and so they can be targets for more intense and direct campaigns by these negative forces in their attempt to lower a child's efficiency and vibration through fear and confusion. I don't think that this "threat" is something that parents of these children should be too concerned about in an immediate way. Remember that a parent being fearful will only perpetuate the cycle of sending out and therefore attracting low level energy beings and this in turn will unnecessarily expose the child to negativity, making them even more vulnerable. What is important to remember and not to discount is that these feelings illustrate that children can be aware of the displeasure their presence causes for certain forces and entities. While I discuss actions parents can take to help protect their child in Chapter 7, insuring that children receive unconditional love and support from their families will make them stronger and allow them to better maintain their vibrational frequency and this is the best protection of all.

It Looks Like God

In November 2000, the kids and I were watching a video called *The Toothbrush Family* that we had taken out from the library. This was a very innocuous and sweet video about the adventures of some bathroom implements. At one point they showed an image which consisted of a lit-up toy house that was set behind a shrub. They showed this image three or four times. One of these "shots" very much resembled an angelic host or being of light of some kind. Upon seeing this, Emmet jumped up and ran to me, hiding behind me. I asked him what was wrong and he explained in a reverent whisper, *"It looks like God, mommy…like God."*

Now this may not appear to be significant, but it is. To begin with the image that Emmet was viewing was nothing like the image we present to children as being what God looks like - an old man with a grey beard and flowing robes - and yet Emmet reacted to it. This illustrates that he was responding from a deep level of knowing and not from a superficial socially-programmed level. The urgency of his reaction illustrates the honesty, the intensity and the depth of his feeling. He took no time to think, but reacted instinctively, as the image appears to have activated a very deep or residual memory within Emmet. And so this simple video led to a little child sharing a beautiful truth – God exists.

Khou-Sa-Heh-Yah

On March 14, 2000 Emmet described and drew a picture of a being that he referred to as Khou-Sa-Heh-Yah. This being had three heads, a tail or two, a sword and a shield upon which Emmet had drawn a cross. He explained that the heads did not have faces "because they don't need faces". He would not tell me too much about this being other than stating emphatically that Khou-Sa-Heh-Yah was mighty and strong, was very good and nice, and was there to serve as a protector of Emmet.

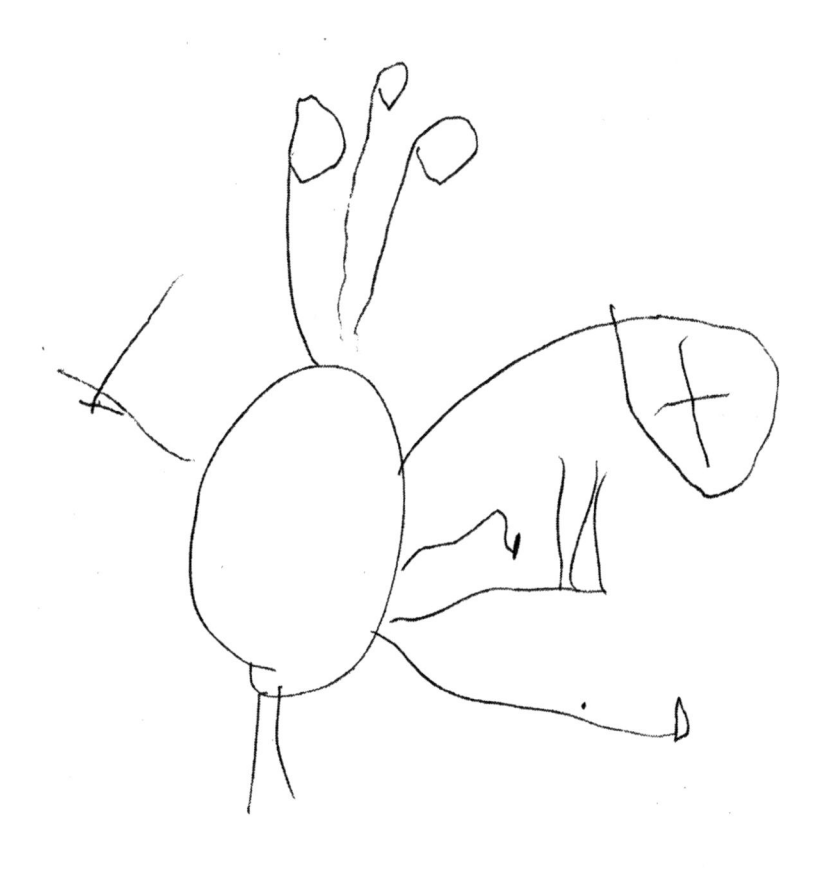

Khou-Sa-Heh-Yah

To see a clearer copy go to www.aknowing.com or to the Facebook page: A Knowing-Living with Psychic Children

As anyone can imagine, I was intrigued and perplexed by this entity that Emmet had described and named. I searched from time-to-time for an entity whose name and description matched this one but was unsuccessful for many years. In August 2003, I thought to look up the words separately, and since they sounded Arabic to me I began to look in that direction and eventually happened upon Ancient Egyptian words. It was here that I had some success with Khou and Sa, but it wasn't until 2009 that I finally discovered the potential meaning of the other words:

Khou –God of Light; similar to the Ka or Ba, which is the essence of the soul[1]

Sa – protection; to protect, to watch over, to take care of[2]

Heh - the God of Infinity and limitless time[3]

Yah – Ancient Egyptian moon god as found in the Papyrus of Ani[4]

(For those that are interested, Ka is the creative intellectual and spiritual power or life force that is sustained by food and drink; Ba is similar to our concept of the soul and is the energy that is our unique personality.)

So Emmet, at the age of four, not only provided a name or description of this entity in an ancient language but his English description of the entity also matched the ancient words he had used. This was a mighty being that was there to provide never-ending protection for my child. I believe that we all have guardian angels, guides and other beings that watch over us and protect us based on need, not just one Guardian Angel. In this instance it seems that one of Emmet's guardians appeared in this specific form for him and conveyed his purpose. It was interesting that when he drew this entity, I was concerned. Despite Emmet's description of Khou-Sa-Heh-Yah as being benevolent, initially I did not like the three heads or the multiple tails, and yet Emmet was quite happy about having seen him and having him by his side as a protector. This is a good example of why it is important to pay attention to what your child says, take your cues from them, and try not to project your own impressions upon them as you may be wrong.

---

1 Dictionary of Ancient Deities; Patricia Turner & Charles Russell Coulter, Oxford University Press
2 Ancient Egyptian Medicine, John Francis Nunn
3 Article – Heh the God of Infinity, Caroline Seawright, touregypt.net
4 A Dictionary of Egyptian Gods and Goddesses, George Hart, Routledge

The Last Monsters

This was a disconcerting picture which Emmet produced in a flurry of output on March 14, 2000 when he put down on paper the many things he had been seeing but had been unable to successfully communicate to me verbally as he lacked the vocabulary to describe the detail. This picture consisted of four beings, which were frightening to Emmet, who were being observed by Jesus who was standing in the corner of the picture, smiling and carrying a sword. He called these four beings "The Last Monsters", and he did not like them at all. When I asked him why Jesus was smiling if the monsters were so bad, he replied, *"Because the monsters are helping Jesus"*. He explained to me that the presence of these "monsters" was going to result in terrible things happening and that this is why Emmet did not like them. He went on to explain that these beings were not really "bad" in and of themselves, and were only doing their job. This job, as terrible as it was, was helping Jesus in some way that he was not able to explain, and this seemed to cause him some distress as well.

The Last Monsters

To see a clearer copy go to www.aknowing.com or to the Facebook page: A Knowing-Living with Psychic Children

It was this picture that I brought to the priest I mentioned earlier on in the book. For Christians, it immediately evokes images of Revelations and The Four Horsemen of the Apocalypse and the priest was not able to provide any explanation for it other than that. It is interesting that up until this point, and ever since this picture, everything that Emmet had expressed in relation to Jesus has been entirely positive, happy, joyous and loving. So this was an anomaly but he was adamant about it. I found it very interesting that a child as young as Emmet could look at these entities and recognize that despite the horror and suffering they would unleash they were not bad or evil in and of themselves but were merely carrying out their assigned job or purpose. It is an eye-opening concept and does much to challenge our concepts of "good" and "evil" as it begs the question, "Does evil really exist? Is there really any such thing or is there a higher purpose for everything that occurs?"

Personally, I believe that anything negative that does happen here is a result of mankind's successive chain of poor and selfish decision-making and behavior, not some arbitrary "punishment" vetted out by specific beings on a particular date, but my opinion is not important here. In terms of Emmet's opinion of this, beyond his horror at what these creatures would bring upon the Earth, he gave no further explanation of why, when, where, etc. For him it just was and it was terrible. I never discussed this with him again because I did not want to cause him any unnecessary upset, but let's hope that as a species we can learn fast and rectify things before we invite this upon ourselves, or rather before we manifest this possibility into being.

The Grid

The following incident speaks to the fact that just because children do not express what they are seeing or experiencing it does not mean that things are not occurring. My son, Connor, is one of those children who does not and will not share things easily or regularly. I try to create and maintain an environment that will allow him to feel comfortable and safe with his experiences and to realize that I am here should he ever decide to share, and this has allowed him to reach out occasionally, as I described in "Jesus' Visit" in Chapter 2. This was not one of those times.

Connor drew a grid one day and the only reason that I even became aware of it was because, uncharacteristically, he drew it on a wall. When I first discovered it, I didn't even understand what it was, but I knew it was something significant. I took pictures of his drawing and showed it to a few people and they all independently agreed with one another that it was a grid, which was something I knew nothing about at the time. Grids function as portals, or doorways, for energy and entities. By their very nature they are there to provide a transfer or facilitate the movement of energy. There are usually two steps involved with grids. The first is drawing the grid and the second is activating it, usually with sound or specific tones delivered in a specific sequence. In the case of Connor's grid it was drawn but never activated, and this was a good thing as it was drawn in anger and so it was prompted by negative energy or beings that he was open to at that specific moment. I would not have wanted to invite any of them in and around us. I have chosen not to include a picture or reproduction of Connor's grid as I would not want anyone to experiment with it. However, I feel that it is safe to include a basic description. This particular grid consisted of an arrow pointing to a door, with another arrow pointing from the door to a being with a pointed tail and an ankh, which is the Ancient Egyptian symbol for life or eternal life. He added to it later and the additional drawings included a clearly drawn (air) craft and a tau cross.

I wanted answers and to try to understand what was occurring, especially how Connor had come to know or be directed to draw this grid. I found it very frustrating that he was unable or unwilling to help me other than to say that he had drawn it while he was very angry, he had been in somewhat of a daze and, in fact, did not really remember drawing it at all, which tells me that it must have come completely through his subconscious. I cannot ever know if this was information that was lying dormant within his subconscious that had been there all along; whether Connor was able to tap into this knowledge at some outside location through his subconscious because of his mental and emotional state at the time; or whether an energy or entity, sensing Connor's negative state of being, directed him through his subconscious to produce this grid. This is the reason why it is so important to insure that a psychic child is protected, feels loved and especially is not allowed to wallow in their negative emotions as this leaves them open to influence or direction by beings or energies that do not have our best interests in mind. In the end, the only thing I could do once I understood what the grid's function was and what prompted its creation, was to insure that any energies and entities related to it had been dealt with and cleared from the house and the land, and then I painted over it.

Grey Lady in the Doorway

In December 2005, Anithe had a nightmare which persisted even in her waking state throughout the day whenever she closed her eyes. Anithe said that she saw a woman standing in an archway which seemed to be elevated, or on a stand. The woman had grey skin and grey hair pulled up into a bun. She was wearing an old fashion style dress which was also grey. There was no light in the archway and so the lady was surrounded by blackness.

This woman was a human being who had become trapped here and wanted help moving on. She had come to Anithe hoping to receive help, but Anithe was not sure how to help her because she was not aware of what this woman wanted or needed. She could see this woman but could not understand what the woman wanted or how to help her, although this woman did eventually move on successfully. Sometimes psychic children are not aware of their abilities or of how to initiate these abilities, and often the children are required to do nothing in particular. In many cases, just being around these children and being exposed to their energy is enough to raise the awareness and vibration of people and beings that are trapped on our plane. These beings are then able to realize themselves where they must go and what they must do without fear or confusion. They recognize that they are blocking themselves and preventing themselves from moving on or returning to where they belong. Once this is realized, they are able to make the transition independently and successfully. It is common in these cases for parents not to be made aware of the presence of these beings.

Because of this gift that psychic children have they can attract many beings, both human and other. These children's energy can be likened to a floodlight beaming out into the darkness, and those who are lost and wandering are drawn to it. It is a beautiful and important job as it not only helps others, it also allows for a clearing of our plane, which is just one more step towards raising the vibration of our Earth and all who are on it to a higher level.

A Friend

Anithe spoke of a nice, blue, male entity that had come to her and had remained around her. She was very fond of this entity and said that they enjoyed doing things together. In the first pictures he was always depicted as crying and had no noticeable aura of energy. In later pictures he is shown smiling with a definite aura emanating from him. This is another being that Anithe, without consciously realizing it, had helped to cross over or move on by allowing him to remain in her proximity to heal. The second picture was drawn right before he left and the positive change in him is obvious with his smile and brilliant aura. Anithe explained that he was able to go home and it makes me happy to know that the reason he "disappeared" is because he was finally able to make his way to where he belonged.

Anithe's friend

To see a clearer copy go to www.aknowing.com or to the Facebook page: A Knowing-Living with Psychic Children

Knowingly and unknowingly these children are affecting positive change in worlds and with beings that are both seen and unseen by us, and that is what all of this is about. So whether they open the mind of a parent or friend thereby raising their awareness and vibration, or help an entity that is invisible to us, or clear a space or area through their presence, these children are precious gifts who should be loved, protected, believed, supported, and honored.

They Are the Letters

Sometimes entities that come around these children looking for help from them can be a bit unusual looking. Again, this is when you have to trust the child's reaction and opinion of them. On May 18, 2001, Emmet handed me pictures of two very odd looking entities. One resembled a snake-like rooster while the other had a tail and a lot of light emanating from him. Emmet had written letters to go with each picture. XRWM was given to the snake-like rooster and TPO was assigned to the other entity. When I asked what these letters meant he replied very seriously, *"the letters are them and they are the letters".*

XRWM

To see a clearer copy go to www.aknowing.com or to the Facebook page: A Knowing-Living with Psychic Children

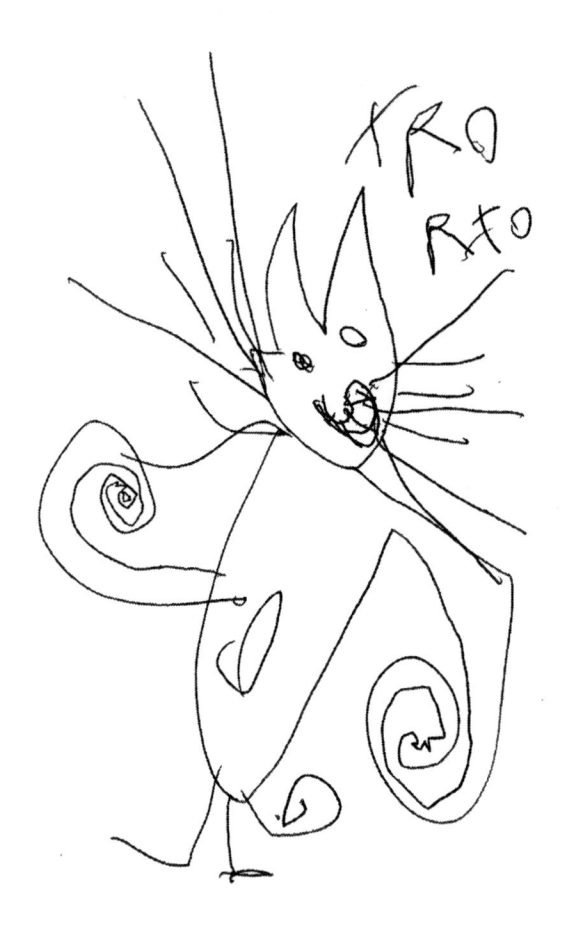

TPO

To see a clearer copy go to www.aknowing.com or to the Facebook page: A Knowing-Living with Psychic Children

While I have to admit that I did not particularly like the look of these two beings, Emmet did not seem concerned about them at all, so I decided to go with his gut instinct and not to become concerned over them. These were entities from another world that had come here and had become trapped. Because of Emmet's type of energy, or light, they had been drawn to him hoping that he could help them return home. The first entity (the snake-rooster) did return home shortly after that. The second entity had great difficulty and required extra help to make the return trip years later which John Collins helped with. Neither of these beings ever caused Emmet any fear or any trouble, and so I am pleased that I did not waste any energy becoming concerned about them.

Seeing Auras

In 2002, we were living in a very difficult situation that caused me a great amount of stress. I tried my best not to show the children that I was distressed and felt that I was doing a good job of covering it, but I never factored in the psychic signs that can't be hidden. On a particularly trying day, I brought the children out into the sun to play. Anithe, who had just turned four, was sitting on a little plastic see-saw staring at me. Finally she said with concern in her voice, "Mommy, there is black all around you!" I was surprised but decided not to question her any further. I merely took note of the fact that she may be seeing auras (of which I knew next to nothing about at the time) and reassured her that the blackness would go away soon.

It wasn't until November 2005, that she mentioned seeing colors around people again. When I asked her why she had not mentioned this previously (she was unaware of the first instance) she said, *"Because I thought everybody could see them."* She went on to explain that since she had always seen auras, she had never thought it was strange, nor had she ever considered that others could not see them. And this is a good point, how can children know to share things with us that we would consider unusual, if they are not aware that they are considered not to be normal? If you have always seen and experienced the world in a particular way, then it is not unusual to you and you will assume that everyone else experiences the world in the same way, and so you will not draw attention to something that you assume others are seeing or experiencing as normal. This is often why children don't mention psychic occurrences...they are not aware that they are psychic! So they assume that other people can see the lady in the corner, or the angel at the foot of their beds but that it is so normal to us that we are just not amused, amazed, or disturbed by them in any way. It is only as they mention things randomly that they begin to realize that perhaps the rest of us perceive the world in a very different and much more limited way!

Guardian Angel

Everyone has at least one Guardian Angel and most children are in touch with them on some level. They may not see them, but they tune into them spontaneously. Children can be encouraged to do this **but be sure to explain that the voice, or information that comes to them, should always be loving and kind and not rude or abusive.** Negative communications should not be entertained under any circumstances regardless of how the entity appears. Should a child share that an entity is expressing any negativity then they should be advised to ignore and block that entity and to ask for extra help and protection from the other side. It will be provided. Space can also be cleared round the child and their environment and a child can learn to erect a psychic shield both of which are covered in Chapter 7. More professional help should be sought should the entity refuse to leave.

My children spoke of and interacted constantly with their Guardian Angels without ever referencing or requiring a name. This seems to be a fairly common phenomenon as it is the adults that require names in order to identify and define all beings and things. Children recognize their angels based on other, more unique and specific indicators, such as feeling, vibration, hues of color, sound and sight. Many angels may reference the same name, but as each of us is an individual, each of them is unique as well and these children identify them from unique qualities that are specific to each one of them. This more accurate way of recognizing entities and angels can change as children venture out and begin to attend school where they are taught that all things must have names in order to be identified. This is the beginning of their indoctrination and of the restriction of their openness and free-thinking nature.

One day in 2002, after Emmet had begun to be influenced by school in little ways but not enough that he had begun to block communication, he told me that he had been sitting in class when he suddenly thought, "What is the name of my Guardian Angel?" The answer came quick and clear, "Her name is Sophie." When he returned home he asked me about this and wanted to know if it was a boy's name or a girl's name and what it meant. When I told him that Sophie was a girl's name he appeared a little disappointed because as a boy I think he fancied the idea of a male warrior who was armed to the teeth and ready to take anything on. However, when I told him that Sophie meant wisdom, he smiled and nodded saying, "That's not bad then." I thought it was interesting that he had been interacting all these years with his Guardian Angels and had never had a need for names from them until the idea or "requirement" had been introduced to him.

I think that beyond showing how our society inadvertently alters the way in which children think, perceive and therefore interact with their environment, it also illustrates why it is so important that children have time to zone out and to go into themselves. Emmet received this information when he was not focused and was daydreaming – to the great annoyance of his teacher, I am sure. We often berate children for not being focused, but I think that we have lost sight of the fact that it is not only necessary for them but that they actually benefit from going into themselves and shutting out the world in order to connect with and seek out the knowing and truths that lie within them and in worlds unseen.

The Inverted Pyramid

On August 28th, 2007, we were sitting on the porch of my parents' house when Anithe saw an inverted pyramid hovering over the neighbor's lawn – all the front lawns are connected so there are no barriers or anything that can cast shadows or odd reflections. This pyramid was purple around the edges and black in the center. She described it as seeming to be larger than it actually looked. In other words, as she looked at it, it appeared to be no bigger than maybe two feet high, but she had a sense that its actual dimensions were far larger than it appeared to her. It was very interesting to hear a young child describe their awareness that what they perceived was not a reflection of the actual reality.

Pyramid Portal

To see this in color go to www.aknowing.com or to the Facebook page: A Knowing-Living with Psychic Children

This sense of knowing that what is being seen is not to scale is not unusual when dealing with psychic phenomena and there is an explanation for this. Keep in mind that whatever is being perceived is something that exists both in its own dimension as well as ours and may be doing so simultaneously. It is not of our dimension, and yet is perceivable from within the third dimension, and so it can be hard to glean an accurate perspective as it relates to our world. Perceptual problems can also come from the fact that within its own dimension, or in its true form, it might appear differently. Also, since what a psychic child is seeing or perceiving has the potential to exist in a different form or state, they can be seeing one "form" while sensing another.

Consider, for example, Pasquale's Guardian Angel in the comic strip *Rose is Rose*. This Guardian Angel mostly takes the form of a cherubic and childlike being but he can transform instantly into a massive, fully-armed, Angelic warrior. I always loved this cartoon as it begs the question, "Which is his true form - the cherub or the imposing warrior?" Is the cherub his true form or just the form this angel projects most of the time in order to appear less threatening and more of a playmate to the child? Does his massive warrior side disappear when he downsizes, or is it still there? Is either form his true form or is he merely able to project and reflect aspects of himself that he wishes to while still maintaining his other forms? Can the child sense all the angel's potential manifestations while only seeing the desired projection? It is this multiplicity of form and being that can cause conflicting and confusing perceptions for a psychic child and it is a challenge that we need to keep in mind as these children struggle to describe to us what it is they know and are experiencing.

Chapter 5
The Dark Side

This chapter comes with a warning because it deals with purely negative experiences and discusses entities and energies that we consider threatening and evil. I structured this book specifically so that it could be read without someone having to go through this chapter. While in the end, there is nothing to fear, people do and there is no point in pretending that we are above this emotion. As I stated before, strong emotion creates strong energy and energy draws similar energy to itself, so if anyone feels that reading about negative beings and situations may cause them to become upset, uneasy, or fearful, please skip this chapter. You can always return to it at a later date. I included this information in the book because these situations do arise and did happen to my children and so they must not be overlooked or avoided because some people may not be ready or able to deal with them. This chapter is specifically included for the benefit and edification of those who are experiencing similar activity in hopes that they take comfort in that they are not alone and that in the end the negative activity around us did in fact, dissipated and we all learned a lot and grew stronger from our experiences. As a parent, I was desperate to try to understand what was going on around my children, and why. As much as I searched I could not find any books that dealt with this issue seriously. Every book was either about positive experiences or had information that was presented in the manner of a scary story told around a campfire or in a sensationalistic way and so I was left even more isolated and wondering what was wrong with us. This did not help our situation at all.

When I was writing this book many people questioned the wisdom of including these events and tried to dissuade me from sharing and I think this is one of the problems with the subject of "evil". Everyone is willing to talk about the positive experiences but very few are willing to deal with the flip side in a serious way, and so there are many parents left searching quietly and desperately for answers. So to avoid causing unnecessary apprehension for others while sharing my children's experience in their entirety, I have provided readers with this warning.

Please do not proceed with this chapter if there is any possibility that it will cause you to fear.

Now for those that have chosen to continue reading or who are dealing with these types of events it is important that you keep in mind that everything is energy – nothing more. I discuss this more in Chapter 6 but basically, the Source provides energy and it is used. Some people and entities use it in positive ways while others do not. But despite appearances and regardless of what it often feels like, evil is not stronger than good, and as nature loves equilibrium there are always ways to balance things out. Try to keep this in mind as you read through our experiences or as you deal with your own issues – evil is just energy that is being used and directed in a specific way.

As I explained earlier, when children are in an environment of love and acceptance, and can sit in a place of love, their energy will vibrate at a higher level. This high level of vibration acts as a protection, as entities and people who vibrate at a lower rate must either raise their own vibration, thus improving and growing, or they must leave the space that the child is occupying. The other option open to those who vibrate at a lower level is to attempt to cause others to come down to their level of vibration. Fear and its many offspring are the most commonly used and are the most effective tools on both this side of the veil and the other side. Everyday human examples would be bullying and criticism, or the threat of violence and abuse. Very basic modes of operation for entities from the other side of the veil may consist of utilizing fearful mental images or ideas, threats, melancholy thoughts and feelings of depression as they hang around and lower the energy within your environment. The purpose of this activity is to lower our ability to vibrate and function as we should which in turn makes us more vulnerable to their influence.

So what types of negative energies or entities would a psychic child be likely to be open to and how vulnerable are they to these dark manifestations? This was a question that concerned me greatly as my children began to see and experience negative things. I have been asked the question, "Why does it matter what they are or what their intentions may be?" because there is a belief that recognizing something gives it identity, power, and validates its existence. This may be true, but as far as I am concerned, they exist already and so in terms dealing with them the answer is simple – I need to know as much as I can. I need to know because I believe that if you understand what you are dealing with, you take away the mystery and, therefore, the fear associated with it. At least that is how I work. For some, knowledge might have the opposite effect, but then the question I would ask is how can you deal with what "ails you" when you do not understand what it is? I find that the more I understand something the more able I am to deal with it and this in itself is empowering. When I am empowered, I do not fear, and so I offer the little knowledge I have acquired through my children regarding negative entities and experiences as an antidote to fear.

Remember that one of the most powerful defenses you have is to sit In-Understanding and in a state Of-Love. The problems negative entities and energies cause and their power over us comes in part because we rarely find ourselves sitting in a state of Understanding and Love. Our lives wear us out and run us down; we work too hard and rest too seldom; we laugh too little and spend too little time with family and friends; we covet material things and so we incur large debts; we make poor decisions; we enter into relationships that drain us; and we engage in behavior that weaken our defenses by lowering our vibrational rate. We also come with baggage that has been handed down to us from family or other children and adults that we have dealt with during our childhood and throughout our everyday life. For those of us who do not posses "the sight" we may think that these beings do not exist or can't effect us, but depression, thoughts of suicide, melancholy, anger, and unexplained fatigue are a few examples of how they do. But can you imagine being able to really sense or actually see these energies and entities? Can you imagine hearing them or knowing their intentions? It must be frightening beyond description, and many of these children are exposed to this reality. As the children fear they become more vulnerable which in turn perpetuates fear and attracts more lower-level energies around them or increases the power of those who are already around them to affect and influence them.

There are countless variations and types of entities that we, as humans, find threatening or "evil" and I cannot pretend to know about all of them, let alone to understand them. I have researched and read to try and compose a picture of these beings for myself. But by far the most insightful overview I was ever given was by John Collins, a marvelous psychic, who spends much of his time clearing negative energies and entities. He works to remove them from places where they have become ensconced and from around people to whom they have become attached. He helps them to return to their homes or to the Source, depending on which is appropriate.

The following is a synoptic overview of what John explained to me. John classifies them into two main groups – those who are from this Earth and those who are not of this world. Read about these entities, and understand that they are present and just as there are humans incarnated upon this planet whose thoughts and deeds do not reflect either love or light there are other, non-human, ones. Do not fear these entities and do not give them undue thought or focus. It is not necessary and will be of no benefit to either you or your family. Read, acknowledge, understand and RELEASE.

Not Of This World

Aliens are an obvious and a good example of this type of entity although I want to emphasize strongly that **most of them are not of evil intent**, as is clearly evident from my children's experiences. Many aliens have our best interests in mind and appear to be doing all they can to help us without direct intervention. I mention them here only because it is evident that some are not benevolent and seem to be engaged in activity that is unacceptable and self-serving.

There are some entities that fall into this category who, as frightening as they may be for those who can see them, are merely here to learn and grow. They would come from a lower vibration or lower levels of development than our own and so they come here for education. They come to observe, experience, and understand and to take that understanding back to their own world to aid in their growth. The fact, however, that they have no negative intent does not mean that they should be allowed to hang around you or your family should they cause any fear or if they are lowering the energetic vibrations of your environment.

There are those whose worlds are dying or are in serious trouble and they enter into our world to take from it or to seed things around us or in our environment with the goal of taking these things back with them. (These can include alien races.) Some are successful in returning with their "treasures" but many get trapped here. Their entry, their attempts at influence and theft are against the rules and their activities are against Universal Law. So while they may gain entry by slipping under the proverbial fence, they have a much more difficult time finding their way back out again and can become trapped. These types use portals for their activities and can cause depression and illness through their presence. (The use of a portal is not indicative of a negative entity or activity. Portals are used for travel by many types of entities.)

Finally there are the demons. They are the Hoards of Hell type that we are most familiar with and are the beings that we believe we are engaged in a great battle with. Most of these entities are lost in the belief that they are not loved or are not worthy of love, something that my son Emmet taught me a few years ago. Their anger and resentment help to fuel their hatred of us and of others who are aware of and maintain their Light that these demons so dearly crave. By choice, through deceit, or by creation they have found themselves in a situation that both excites and causes them to fear. In terms of their interactions with humans, I believe the saying, "Misery loves company," would best describe their motivations. I am not sure that they operate under the idea that the "side" with the most players wins, but they certainly seem to believe that they gain individual power through the influence and control of the energy of others. When thinking or dealing with these entities remember that all creation, all that exists, contains a spark of Light within it. This is the Light of God that is required for all things to exist. The knowledge that we are all sparks of beautiful light, of energy that is the Source, can help raise us all up, and we should keep it in mind when we look at these beings because it can be easy to cover up our brilliance and then forget who we are - whether we are human or not.

Of This Earth

Negative energies that we as individuals and as a race have created through negative thoughts, emotions and actions are extremely prevalent. These energies can be a result of a war or other massive atrocity or they may be a result of individual cruelty and suffering, beginning as small and insignificant but increasing in size and growing in strength over time. This growth occurs in two ways that I am aware of. The first is by attracting and combining with other similar energies. Think of mercury and how it is drawn to and merges easily with separated parts of itself and you have the idea. Energy will attract like to like, and left to its own devises it can grow to a point where its mere presence perpetuates the same negative emotion, thinking, and actions that spawned it into existence…and so it will continue to exist and gain in effectiveness and power. The second way is similar to the first but involves attaching or focusing on a particular individual to provide it with energy and power. The energy "hangs around" attempting to affect the individual's state of mind and being so as to stimulate more negativity. We are responsible for creating and perpetuating these negative energy beings, but we are also the ones that can starve them of their supply and replace their space with beautiful and loving positive energy.

The second type of entity in this category would be human beings who became extremely distorted in their thought and emotion during their time on Earth. This is not to judge or condemn them in any way as they, like each of us, have the ability to change and alter that thought pattern and heal their emotional state. Until they do, however, they can cause extreme problems. Despair and depression surround them and they can sometimes take the specific form of what John refers to as "soul-collectors" (but who I will refer to as Energy-Collectors), who trick and trap people in order to feed off their energy and life force like a parasite. They should not be left to hang around anyone for any reason. An unexplained bad smell can sometimes accompany an Energy-Collector and can be a hint of their presence.

As you can imagine, having the ability to see these beings can be very frightening indeed, especially for young children. As he began to see and sense these entities Emmet even became afraid of going anywhere in our house on his own. He was able to be alone in a room if someone else was on the same floor as he was, but he would not go downstairs or upstairs if no one else was there. Anithe, 2 ½ years his junior, began to take on the responsibility of accompanying him when he was concerned about being alone. This was extremely sweet and often funny and allowed for greatness of heart during a very stressful time. I remember the first time Anithe realized that Emmet was afraid to go places on his own. Emmet wanted to get a toy from upstairs, but I was in the middle of making dinner and couldn't go with him at that precise moment. Being young and eager to play he did not want to wait for me to finish cooking. Anithe looked up at him and said confidently, "Don't worry Emmet. I will come and protect you!" She led him toward the staircase holding his hand. I watched them as she climbed the stairs on all fours in her t-shirt and little diaper and encouraged Emmet to follow her, assuring him the entire way that all would be well. It was hilarious and heart-warming. From that point until Emmet's negative experiences began to subside and he became less wary, she was his companion and protector on excursions into any "empty" zone and she took this responsibility quite seriously.

Having lived with a child who could perceive these negative beings, I do realize that it can be a huge strain to have to accompany them to places when you perceive no need. But for them, the need is there and is as real as anything in their lives. If we could see what they can we would not allow them to enter these spaces without support and protection. We provide protection through our presence, our reassurance, and our love. This allows the child the ability to protect themselves through their aura and through their belief that they cannot be hurt by these entities and energies in any way. A child's belief in their invulnerability and absolute protection is very important because thought is energy and thought combined with emotion produces great power. Do not try to discount their insistence that there are monsters as this is not helpful in the least and, in fact, can cause them even more stress as they can clearly see, hear, or sense them. It amounts to calling the child a liar or highlighting to them that their parent is not aware of these beings and is therefore not able to provide protection. You do not need to confirm or deny that you can see or sense what they are reporting to you, just place the focus on the child and what they saw or experienced and try your best to reassure them that these monsters won't hurt them. The more you can dispel fear and reinforce the idea that they are protected, the better off they will be. If you are pushed as to whether or not you can perceive these things, never lie. You can honestly tell them that some people can perceive these things and others cannot, that it is a gift or a talent like being good at kicking a ball or singing, and that the child is good at perceiving these beings and that you are not but *that your talent is being good at protecting them.* Children understand this and will take great comfort from it.

The Black Doorway

When Emmet was 5, he began seeing what he described as a black doorway in his room that appeared just below the area of the ceiling. He asked that I open it to see what was behind it or in it because he felt very uncomfortable about it and was afraid of what might come out of it. I thought it was interesting that he did not realize that I could not see it or that it was not a tangible object within this dimension. This clearly demonstrates that there is little to no difference in a psychic child's perception of things that come from our dimension and those that come from elsewhere – it is all real to them. The door remained for a period of time and I was unable to think of anything I could do to get rid of it. Finally, in desperation, I held him in my arms and told him that nothing could really hurt him, that he was loved and safe, and that if he wanted help he should ask for protection himself. I explained that he could ask God or Jesus to remove the door. He thought about it for a few minutes, then closed his eyes and was quiet for a while before getting up and running off. I waited until bedtime to ask about the door. He looked up and smiled, telling me it had gone and instead there were clouds that emitted multi-colored light. These clouds and light followed him around on and off for a while afterwards and I was relieved that Emmet seemed happy and unafraid and that the black door did not return. I was later to discover that these clouds and multi-colored lights were angels, and I am grateful to this day that these angels responded to his plea.

As anyone can imagine, until the doorway disappeared, this was a very disconcerting experience for him. I now know that this doorway was a portal through which, I am sure, many entities gained access or intended to gain access to our world and to our home. However at the time I knew nothing about portals, what they were for, or how to get rid of them. I only knew that a black doorway on the ceiling was probably not a positive thing and that I didn't want it there.

More importantly than whether or not this portal was "functional", this doorway placed Emmet into a state of fear and distraction, lowering his vibration and mine as it weighed heavily on us, preoccupying our daily thoughts and affecting our emotional state. The lesson I learned from this incident was extremely important, and yet it was a lesson that I was not to understand immediately. When Emmet first mentioned this doorway, fear and a sense of helplessness took over. Both of us sat in this place of fear and victimization until Emmet received confidence from me that he himself was able to rectify the situation and to affect change. When Emmet's efforts were successful and the door disappeared, I merely went from fear to relief – the lesson passing me by. This is not unusual. It often takes time and distance before we can attain perspective and properly see and understand what the message or lesson was. The lesson I finally realized was simple. *Put ego aside, step away from fear, then ask and you shall receive.* The incident placed us both in a position of being fearful and feeling powerless and from it we learned that the power of change lies within all of us - all we need to do is sit in a state Of-Love, believe, and know that help is there and that there are agents of the Light that are willing and able to help us when we need help and reach out for it. We are never alone and we don't necessarily need anyone else, like a psychic or a priest, to facilitate our requests. But we must believe, we must have confidence and know without doubt that the help is there and that we are worthy of that help and support. So for all the panic, questions, anger, and frustration all it took in the end was for Emmet himself to ask for help. This is something that we, as parents, need to keep in mind – these children can help themselves and we must help them to become empowered and confident in their ability to manage their gifts. Children are very connected to all, especially the Light, and their calls for help are quickly answered.

Bad Smells

Bad smells are never indicative of something positive. As with the ability to see entities, not everyone will smell these odors. These psychic smells can be detected even if the child is completely congested, as was the case in early March 2001 for Emmet. At the time he was suffering from enlarged adenoids and continuous sinusitis, and was rarely if ever capable of smelling anything at all.

I had just given the three of them a bath and I had moved them into my room in order to dress them when Emmet became extremely upset, his hands flew up to his nose, and he demanded to know what the terrible smell in the room was. Neither I nor the other two kids could smell anything out of the ordinary. At first I dismissed this, but his persistence about the smell, his fear, and his complete and uncharacteristic refusal to be distracted from this situation through play made me think that perhaps something psychic was occurring. I checked anything that could have had a bad odor, including the fresh towel I had wrapped around him, but I could find nothing. As the smell persisted, Emmet became more panicked and wanted to get out of my room. I took them all downstairs at which point he seemed to calm down a little. He told me that he was not able to describe the smell but that he had never smelled anything like it before and that it was "horrible". He stayed very close to me all evening, and when I read them a story that night by the fire, I noticed him glancing uncomfortably over his shoulder several times. Suddenly his face changed expression and he quickly slipped to the floor closer to me where he said he thought he would be "safe". He would not explain what he thought he needed to be safe from or what he had seen or sensed that made him so feel that he was under threat and I did not ask him. I merely reassured him that he was safe and held him close.

As I mentioned earlier, it is only a very negative entity that creates this horrible psychic smell – the smell of decay and death – and it is often the Energy-Collector that I describe earlier in this chapter. These are entities that become stronger by feeding off the energy of others. According to John, they encourage depression and sadness by remaining close and attaching to us with the eventual goal of persuading individuals to commit suicide. If the targeted person should make the decision to commit suicide, then the Energy-Collector, through the application of fear and deceit, will *attempt* to "collect" and feed off of the energy of that person by keeping them close. *(Please note that more often than not they are not successful in their attempts.)* This activity is against Universal Law, or the Law of God, and they have absolutely no right to engage in this activity, but they do. I cannot be sure that this is indeed the type of entity that was in our house that night, but suffice it to say that whatever Emmet smelled and saw that evening must have been extremely unpleasant and terrifying for him, and it was only made worse by the fact that he alone was aware of this entity's presence.

I want to make the point that these children are extremely brave. I cannot state this emphatically enough. I know that I would be unable to face the many things that my children have without falling apart completely. I am in awe of their courage and strength and cannot emphasize enough that they require love and support and should not be belittled or brushed off.

Aku

When Emmet began having psychic experiences at the age of four, he did not have the ability or vocabulary to explain what he was seeing and experiencing so I asked him to draw them instead. He sat down and proceeded to draw 11 pictures of various entities, some of which were bad, and then explained what they were and answered my questions about each drawing. He drew what I would have considered some very frightening beasts including one he referred to as Aku. Aku was the only entity he drew in color on that day, which made him stand out.

Aku

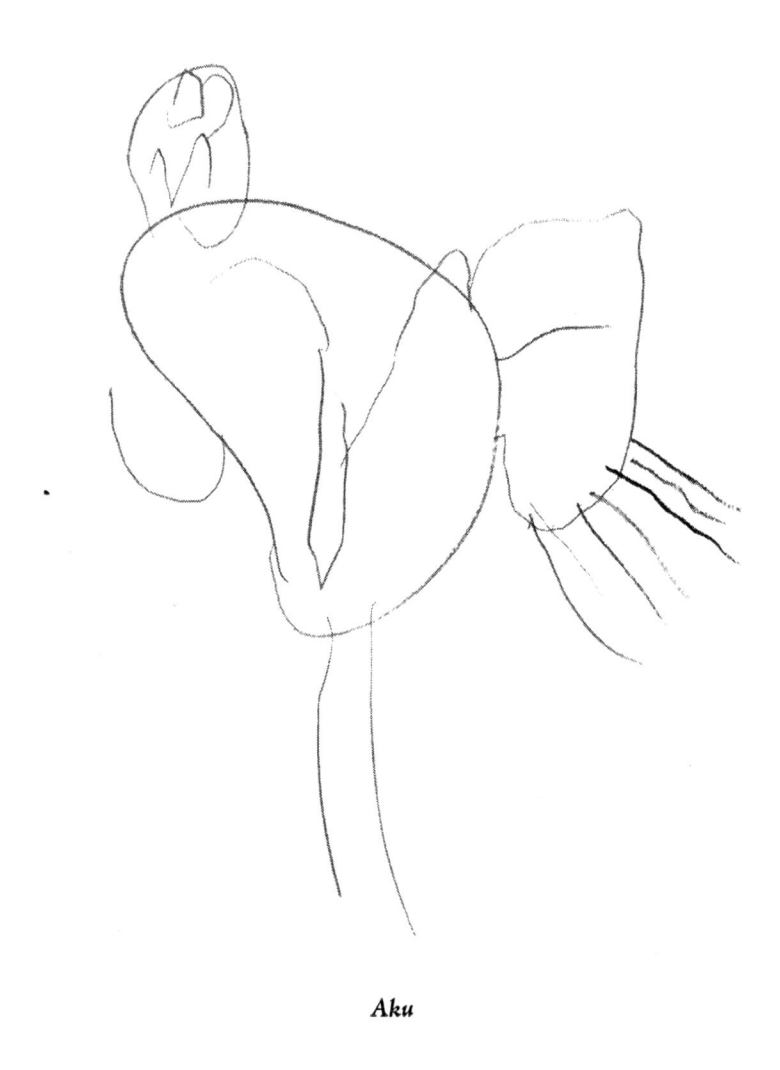

To see this in color go to <u>www.aknowing.com</u> or to the Facebook page: A Knowing-Living with Psychic Children

Emmet disliked this entity intensely and showed obvious fear when discussing him. He said, "He is a bad guy with wings. I saw him when I was a baby (and I was) running around looking for someone. He was stealing gold." This reference to gold is very interesting as it is extremely significant in its symbolism. Gold represents the soul or that part of us that is Divine. So this entity was stealing or attempting to steal both from us and from God what can only be claimed by God.

As I outlined in the first few pages of this chapter, I have come to understand that some lower-vibrating, or "negative" entities that exist were human beings at one stage; some are man-made, created through our intense emotions, activities, and mass consciousness; while others are not of our world but either pre-date mankind or come from other dimensions. Aku was not of this Earth and is of a type that utilizes portals to enter and exit from here. They are not here on holiday or out of curiosity. Entities like Aku are here for the specific purpose of taking from us or planting/seeding things within our plane without permission and against Universal Law. So despite his colorful "tail" he is no angel. Thankfully Emmet never spoke about Aku again, but throughout the years he would see many other entities that, like Aku, appeared to be stealing or collecting gold.

Doesn't Belong Here

Being open to the psychic world obviously has its downside. Children can receive negative feelings, messages and interact with negative entities the same way as they can with those of the Light. The former type of interaction can be distressing for the child as well as for the parent, especially as a young child may not have the vocabulary to explain exactly what is occurring, while the parent may be at a loss as to how to manage or protect the child from this type of interaction. Emmet had many of these episodes, where he sensed something wished him ill. These began in 2000, when he was four years old. This type of feeling had dogged Emmet and by September 29, 2003 he became overwhelmed by it, bursting into tears as he shared that he felt strongly that whatever did not want him here wanted to harm or kill him.

"I get this feeling at night that I shouldn't be here. I feel that something doesn't want me here, and that scares me. I feel as if I should be in another world. I feel as if the thing that doesn't want me here wants to kill me and that's what makes me scared." -E

He felt that this negative attention and focus on him had something to do with his job, or mission, and whatever was focused on him wanted to stop him from completing it. He, of course, had and still has no idea of what this mission or job specifically is. The feeling of helplessness as a parent in this situation is terrible, but is nothing in comparison to what the child must be feeling. I mention this because it is real and not imaginary. It is not an attempt by the child to get attention and they should not be brushed off. Parents should place themselves in the situation of the child and ask themselves what they would require to feel secure if they themselves were being watched or stalked by someone who they did not know and whose intentions they could not ascertain other than that the stalker wished them harm. We would want to be believed, we would want support and love and we would want some assurance of protection. We would not want to be ignored, or told we were imagining things. We would not want to be informed that there was nothing anyone could do until the stalker actually assaulted us and we would not want to be laughed at. So we, as the guardians and protectors of our children, must afford them at least as much consideration and respect as we would look for ourselves. Luckily, in addition to our support and love there is Divine help available for this real situation. In this realm we have the police to deal with stalkers and those individuals who break the law. For the realms beyond the veil we have Angels and other entities of the Light who perform the same function but with far more effectiveness.

It's important to realize that, except for one instance, Emmet was never hurt by these particular entities in a physical or direct way, they just lurked around him from time to time making him fearful. They did not have the right or the ability to approach him or to bring about negative events in his life because he was protected.

Choose Between Light & Dark

One of the most upsetting and disconcerting events that occurred with Emmet began on April 10, 2001. Despite not being religious at the time, the events that had occurred over the past year had shaken me tremendously. In desperation I bought a few rosaries to place by the children's beds in hopes that it might stave off some of the bizarre experiences that were occurring. On April 10, 2001 at 8 p.m. Emmet picked up his rosary and gazed at it. I asked him what he was doing.

"I'm confused. I'm trying to decide." -E

"Decide what, love?" -CP

"Decide if I love God and Jesus or not." -E

"What do you mean Emmet? Don't you love God and Jesus?" -CP

"I don't know...I'm confused." -E

"Why are you confused?" -CP

"They said that I could love God and Jesus, or not love them." -E

"Who said that?" -CP

"The monsters...Mommy, I'd rather not have to choose."-E

To say that my blood ran cold at this point would be an understatement. The concept of having a choice, especially about this issue, is a very adult one and one that many of us do not even give thought to – it is just assumed that most of us would turn to the Light. For a child of four to bring it up as a real and tangible decision was overwhelming to me. I was filled with a sense of fear and anger that a child would be allowed to be faced with such a situation at such a young age. I was also angry that he was being allowed to feel afraid of wanting to choose the Light by these entities. To be honest, I felt that both the request and the circumstances under which this demand was being made were grossly unfair to say the least. In retrospect I do not believe that Emmet was ever in any real danger of being frightened into making the wrong choice as I believe that choices of this magnitude must be made freely and from the heart, but at that time in the middle of this situation, I was terrified and extremely angry.

I remained as calm as I could and explained about the goodness of God and how good always wins and is the Light, while the monsters were Darkness. I told Emmet the he should not listen to the monsters because they were lying in order to trick him into making the wrong choice so that both Emmet would be "sad" and that God would be "sad". Emmet's response was merely to repeat that he did not want to have to choose. I let the matter drop and proceeded to tell two bedtime stories. The first one was completely "off-topic" while the second one was a very for-children version of the Garden of Eden. I was hoping to help Emmet understand what choice he needed to make without directly discussing the matter. I explained how Adam and Eve were tricked by a monster named Lucifer who told them lies and gave them empty promises. I explained that when Adam and Eve broke their word to God they felt very sad and had to leave Eden because the garden had been ruined by the lies and the breaking of their word to God. I explained that God still loved Adam and Eve very much and was very sad about them having to leave the Garden, and that He promised that when they died they would go to Heaven so that they could all be together again, and be happy. I also explained that God promised that He would send Jesus to Earth to correct the mistakes that Adam and Eve had made and that this would help everybody. Emmet listened to the story intently. He then put the rosary on and said, "*I think I choose God and Jesus.*" I breathed a quiet sigh of relief.

The Man Who Destroyed God

This incident occurred on December 3, 2000. I had sent Emmet to his room for being "bold" but as he was so young I followed quickly after him in order to be sure that he was not too upset. I intended to wait outside the doorway and was going to go in to speak with him after about a minute or two. As I stood outside his door, I heard him having a conversation with someone. I could only hear his side of the conversation. There were probable pauses between his responses as if giving time to another to speak. Emmet was vehemently stating that he would not do whatever was being suggested to him. He was saying, *"No! I won't do that...it's not nice!"* Again, it was not so much what he was saying as how he was saying it with such conviction and emotion. Confused, I quickly entered the room. I asked Emmet who he was talking to.

"I was talking to a man." –E

"What man?" –CP

"The man who destroyed God." –E

    I went over to him, picked him up in my arms and brought him directly out of the room and downstairs. I gave him a piece of paper and asked him to draw this man that he had been speaking to, which he did.

The Man Who Destroyed God

To see this in color go to www.aknowing.com or to the Facebook page: A Knowing-Living with Psychic Children

I was struck that this drawing looked almost like a medieval depiction of the Devil. As a tester of his depiction, I asked him if this was a dragon. He was quite disgusted at my lack of artistic appreciation, and so he drew a dragon for me so that I could see the difference. They were not at all alike. Attempting to remain as calm as I could, I explained that no one had or could destroy God so therefore this man he was speaking to was not telling the truth and was not to be trusted. I asked Emmet never to speak to him again, and to come and get me straight away if he ever saw this "man" again. Emmet assured me that he would follow my request.

The Attack

It was this incident that occurred in October of 2000 that proved to me that what my children were experiencing was not imagination. It is unfortunate that this incident was a physical one as these types of situations bring the level of emotion from fear to absolute terror, even if it is only momentary, and they cause physical pain. I am thankful that it was the only time in my children's lives that any entity or energy was able to breach their protection completely.

I was reading to the children in my daughter's room. My two sons sat on either side of me while my daughter sat on my lap. We read two fairly long stories. When we finished I asked Anithe to wait for me in her bed while I brought the boys into their room, which was next to hers. Connor and Emmet were walking ahead of me, and my husband was waiting in the room to help put them to bed. My husband was standing in the room in line with the doorway and so he too was able to witness what happened next. Connor entered the room and walked toward his bed. Emmet entered the room and took two or three steps. Suddenly, he flinched with pain and grabbed his side screaming, "*Stop! It hurts! It hurts!*" He was really in agony and distress. My husband and I rushed to him, and thinking that there may have been something in his pajamas stinging him or biting him, we began to strip off his clothes, pat them down and check his body for anything unusual while trying to comfort him and tell him everything was alright. We found nothing in his p.j.'s that could have caused him any pain. Turning our full attention to Emmet we found that he had large marks that were developing both in the front and back of his torso. They almost looked like something with very large hands had gripped him and squeezed. There were three marks to the front and two to the back, and they were fresh. I watched as they became redder and redder before my eyes. It was nearly impossible to console Emmet, as can be imagined. I stayed with him all night and held him close to me. The next morning the marks were turning horrible colors and I was so concerned that I took him to our doctor. After examining Emmet the doctor said it was a "trauma", that it would take a while to heal and would turn quite ugly looking but that there was no serious physical damage. He could not explain how Emmet could have sustained such an injury under the circumstances that I described to him, but I give our doctor a lot of credit for not making me feel as if I was insane. The bruise eventually became purplish-black and yellow and took weeks to fade. It took a lot longer for the experience to fade for Emmet and for me.

For any parent who has experienced something like this, my heart goes out to you and your child. Thankfully it is rare. I dealt with it by praying and demanding that Emmet and my other children be protected from these attacks and that this situation should never occur again, and by trying to assure and give enough love and support to Emmet in hopes that his sense of vulnerability would be replaced by a sense of security. My husband dealt with it by acknowledging that what had occurred was terrifying and mystifying, but insisted that there must be a logical explanation for it. He then disengaged from it and the "logical" explanation was never forthcoming from him. He does not like to discuss the situation at all.

This being was a man-made entity that grew from negative human emotion. Negative human emotion gave it life and negative human emotion kept it alive and strong. Why it chose to attack Emmet is a mystery. Was it because it required negativity and fear to sustain itself or grow? Was it because Emmet was merely the one who was most open to it at that time? Was it because there was something about Emmet it despised or wished to crush? Was Emmet, through his presence and light, unknowingly helping other beings to heal and return home, depriving this energy-entity of further power? Or perhaps it was to serve as proof beyond any doubt that these events that were occurring with the children were not fantastical. We may never know, but because these children are here to raise energy vibrations and consciousness and to help us to heal and grow emotionally and spiritually, they can be targets of negativity. The important thing is to keep a shield of love and protection around your children, and to try to deal with familial situations quickly in order not to allow negative or resentful emotions to permeate and linger in your home acting as a beacon to unwanted entities and energies.

Confusing Communications: A Fearful Smokescreen

On April 16, 2003 Emmet attempted to share something he had received that he felt concerned about. He also drew a picture of the entity associated with this message and it was this drawing that, in the end, provided the answer to what was occurring.

I'm feeling very sad, but I don't know why. It has something to do with the letter K...but it's not kill. King? Maybe not a king, maybe a president... something to do with a president." –E

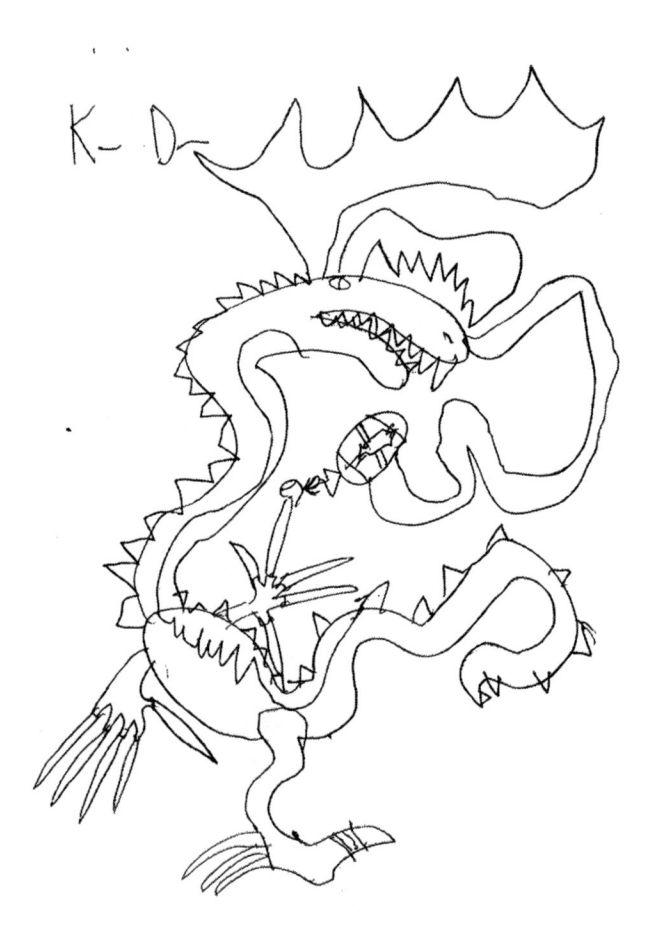

Demon

To see a clearer copy go to <u>www.aknowing.com</u> or to the Facebook page: A Knowing-Living with Psychic Children

Putting the message aside for a moment, this picture obviously depicts a demon. Their job is to keep individuals like Emmet out of the equation by distracting them and putting them into a state of fear or confusion, which is low energy. So even if they cannot harm these children directly or ally themselves with them, they can attempt to nullify the child's energy and positive contribution. The message in this case is meaningless but it does have power if we allow it to. The more we ponder it and focus on it the more the demon is able to focus its attention on the energy of the person who is considering it and the same goes for wallowing in the low emotion its presence evokes in us. The longer this goes on for, the sharper the demon's focus becomes on us and so we become an easy target. This may his game but it is up to us as to whether or not we decide to play and we can chose not to. *"I'm feeling very sad, but I don't know why."* This statement was a key indicator to the presence of a negative entity. Looking at the depiction, there is an appendage that extends from its nose and acts as a vacuum that attaches to us and that sucks or drains our energy leaving us feeling tired and sad without any obvious reason. So this demon acted as an emotional leech as well. It was only luck that at that time there was so much going on that we did not spend undue time and focus on it and, therefore, did not engage with it in any meaningful way.

Once you have looked at a message or feeling that has been communicated to you by your child, and any picture or description of the being that transmitted it, you need to make a decision. Is it worth pondering about and does it have significance? How does it make you feel – fearful? Is there any hope in the message? Is it a warning or is it a threat? Don't spend too long obsessing on this and remember to follow your gut instinct. If the experience is similar to this one, then let it go and turn to your Guardian Angels and those of your child and ask for protection and help. Be as specific as you can in terms of what you want them to do and the situation you wish them to rectify. It is of the utmost importance that we actively invite our Guardian Angels back into our lives as it empowers both them and ourselves. If you wish you can also invoke and call in the Archangels – it never hurts to have a seriously powerful back-up force! This is what we did and to the best of my knowledge this demon never appeared again and none of the children ever received any more messages or feelings from him.

"Ghoul" in the Black Cloak

By the summer of 2002, I found there was a particular entity that had been persistently hanging around and showing itself to Emmet. He appeared in Emmet's dreams as well as making continued appearances while Emmet was awake until well into the spring of 2003. Emmet found him threatening and yet he never seemed to "do" anything. As you can see from Emmet's depictions, he was a frightening being and so, despite the fact that he did not cause harm, angelic intervention was eventually requested and this entity departed.

Ghoul in the Black Cloak

To see a clearer copy go to www.aknowing.com or to the Facebook page: A Knowing-Living with Psychic Children

From what I understand, this type of being is from a lower and different vibration than ours and comes here to observe and to learn rather than to cause harm or discord. Their lower bodies act as tentacles that "feel" the emotion and the interactions that are occurring around them. They are not watchers in the way that aliens or higher beings have been described as watchers. They are not here for our benefit, they are here for themselves and their own edification and development. The problem is that it can be extremely disconcerting to have one of these sitting in your house, tentacles reaching out, saying nothing and just watching… especially if you are the only one who can see them. Their presence can instill fear which regardless of their intentions is not acceptable, and this is what was occurring with Emmet. Their lower vibration can affect the overall energy of the house and so they can have a negative effect on people's emotions and energy levels despite the fact that their intent may not be negative.

Emotional & Energy Leeches

Children are very open to emotion – positive and negative – and they can often see and feel these emotions in very real ways. They can also perceive the entities that move in to encourage negativity and those that merely benefit from naturally occurring conflicts and emotional upheaval. One way that these negative emotions and feelings are tapped is through a psychic cord that extends directly from the entity or demon to a human host. Our energy flows towards these beings giving them power and strength – rejuvenating them. The picture below is of a man who has had an argument, has been fuming and has allowed his anger to fester. He is perpetuating his own negativity by not allowing himself to forgive, and is leaving himself open and vulnerable to negative entities and energies. As is evident from the picture this man has either attracted a negative entity or has allowed an entity that was already hanging around him in tap into his output of negativity and energy.

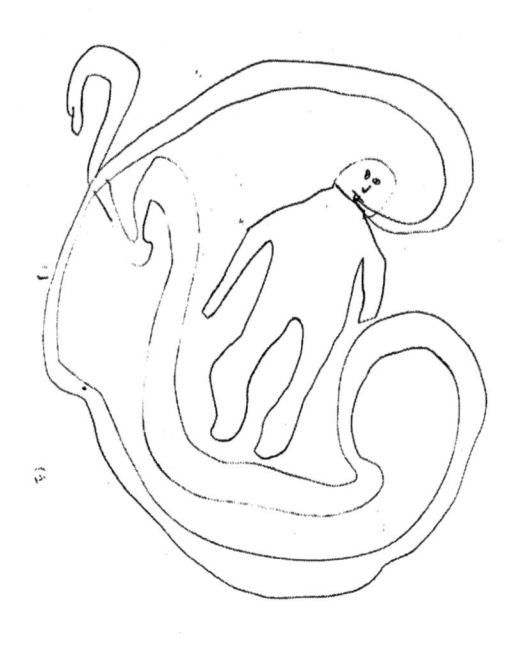

Human Host

To see a clearer copy go to www.aknowing.com or to the Facebook page: A Knowing-Living with Psychic Children

As if the picture of the man was not disturbing enough, Emmet also drew the entity that was attached to the other end of the cord.

Energy-Leeching Entity

To see a clearer copy go to www.aknowing.com or to the Facebook page: A Knowing-Living with Psychic Children

As can be clearly seen, this type of entity is equipped with a cord that extends out from its body, in this case from the area of the stomach or torso - it is not a tail. I found him scary when I first saw him, but the point of all of sharing all of this is not to frighten but to educate, and grow.

We all have arguments and we all become angry. It would be fairly ridiculous to expect people not to experience negative emotions. But the point is not to hold onto them, whatever they are. Deal with the situation,

121

experience the negative emotions (if it can't be helped) and then let it go by forgiving yourself and others and then sit back into a state Of-Love. Call your angels to cleanse you and to cut any cords of negativity that may have formed between you and another person or with an entity that may be draining your energy. Step back from the situation when you are at peace and try to understand what happened and why – try to see if there is a message or a lesson you need to recognize. If negative emotion returns, then perhaps it is a situation that is manifesting in order to put you over the edge, or perhaps it is just too soon for the lesson to reveal itself. Let it go. Above all don't let fear, anger, jealousy, hate or any other negative feeling fester or you may find yourself in a situation similar to the man in that picture.

Bellowing

If you are not particularly psychic, it will be unusual for you to experience things when your children do. This is probably a good thing as we, the parents, are supposed to remain strong, imparting a sense of love and protection to our children, not squealing like stuck pigs or shaking with fear. Every once in a while, however, we are given the "opportunity" to experience along with them. Not to seem like a coward, but I, for one, am appreciative that I have not shared too many of these experiences as I don't feel that I am particularly well equipped to deal with them.

On October 26, 2001 I was unable to sleep, and so I lay in bed reading. At 5:30 a.m. I heard the sound of little feet moving fast and Emmet came running into my room. He was afraid but did not want to explain why. He climbed into bed with me, and despite my reassurances that he was safe, he insisted that he would not go to sleep. No sooner had I got him to calm down a little bit, we both heard an extremely loud sound that could only be described as an angry or frustrated bellowing that Emmet aptly likened to the sound a dinosaur might make (they loved dinosaur documentaries). There was a low pitch, a higher pitch, and a low pitch again. Then silence. We looked at each other and he held onto me even tighter. I strained to listen but there was no other sound. I told Emmet to cuddle into his father, who had not been disturbed by the noise, and I ran down to check my other children as the sound had come from that area of the house. They were both sleeping peacefully which was something that neither Emmet nor I were to achieve for the rest of the night. I looked out of the windows and searched their area of the house but I found nothing. I cannot explain what this was but I can say with confidence that it was not the heating or the boiler or anything else I could think of. It sounded like it came from a huge angry animal. I never heard this sound again.

Ask, Listen and Raise Them Up

On April 17, 2001 Emmet woke up in a terrible mood, which was very uncharacteristic. Normally he was very upbeat and engaged with everyone. He would look for cuddles, pass out toys and play with our new puppy. On this morning he would not talk to anyone, he closed his door and wanted to be left alone. I went into the room to talk to him thinking that perhaps he had fought with one of his siblings. Besides denying that there had been a conflict, he resisted explaining what had put him into this withdrawn state. It is important to remember that often these children will keep things from you for your own protection. They don't want to frighten or upset you and so they try to be brave and deal with these psychic occurrences themselves. But with a little persistence and cajoling I eventually got him to talk about what was bothering him.

Emmet explained that he had had a bad "dream" (dreams are not always dreams, it is often a way children refer to things they experience or see that are from other dimensions) involving a type of monster he had not seen before, but that he did see again at a later date. He explained that while he was not involved in the dream, he was observing the activity. He told me that he had observed many of these beasts flying around where he was. They had two horns on their head, one horn on their nose, four arms, two legs and two wings. Some were breathing fire, some were flying, while others were picking up gold. Just as a reminder, gold is representative of our souls, or that part of us that is Divine. The picture on the left was drawn on that day. The picture on the right was drawn a few years later when Emmet saw them again.

Flying Monsters: Gold Collectors

To see a clearer copy go to www.aknowing.com or to the Facebook page: A Knowing-Living with Psychic Children

These are beings who chose terrible paths while they were incarnated and they therefore became distorted both in thought and in form (as one follows the other). It is important to remember that this is the result of a lack of love and forgiveness that perpetuates negativity that eventually results in distortion. We are not usually able to see the results of such negative thoughts and deeds on our human forms because we are in such a solid physical state but the effect upon the energy-body is huge. Remember that what these children perceive is symbolic because they are not seeing an actual, physical, solid form, but rather are perceiving energy. The way we decipher and "read" energy is through symbols and representations, which is another reason why the perception can change between individuals – symbols and vibrations will often have different meaning to different people. It is also the reason why these entities are sometimes so very bizarre looking – their energy is being deciphered symbolically.

These particular entities were trying to steal the energy of the Light as their thoughts have become so dark that they are not able to see or recognize their own Light. They are not aware that the Light of the Source, or God, exists within them and they do not realize that they can access it, so they look to the Light of others and act either as leeches or as thieves. Ironically, if they would merely recognize the Divine within themselves they could regain their original form as the beautiful beings that they are and could return to the Source. These entities will often pick a weak spot around us and attempt to use others to reach that weakness. Even a seemingly positive statement from someone can deal an emotional blow if they push a sensitive button for us. For example, a person who has achieved success in an area that their parents do not approve of could experience emotional distress if someone compliments them by saying, "Oh, your parents must be so proud of you." A whole Pandora's Box of old emotion and flashbacks to conflicts can flood through a person from a single well-meaning statement such as that. And this is great news for these types of entities who can then move in closer and perpetuate feelings of sadness or worthlessness in order that they become stronger and "feed" off our energetic output without resistance.

Part of why these children have come here is to combat this sort of thing and to clear the energy surrounding us and our Earth and they often accomplish this without even realizing what they are doing. This can be tiring for them and can require contemplation. Quiet time, down time, time to day dream – these periods of non-activity are extremely important for them if they are to succeed in their tasks and recover from their efforts. They will also go into themselves and seek solitude when they are dealing with or have dealt with psychic defense or clearing of a space and this solitude should be respected. If you feel concerned about them, just give them a hug and remind them that you love them and that you are there for them no matter what it is that they need. This will provide them with any added strength and support they may require. So ask question, listen openly, provide them with love and support and help these children to raise themselves up through the strength of their own Light.

Cat-Faced Leader

On May 17, 2001 I was reading on my bed to Connor and Emmet after having put Anithe to sleep, when suddenly Emmet jumped out of his skin with fear, grabbed me around the waist and asked me if I had "seen that". He was so concerned by what he saw that he insisted that I leave the two of them on their own in order to check on Anithe who was sleeping in the area of the house that he saw this monster walking toward. I did as he requested and returned to assure him that his sister was alright. He was still so concerned that he insisted that I move her to the guest room that was adjacent to my room, which I did. I then handed Emmet paper and a pen and asked him to draw what he had seen.

The first beast he drew was the one he had just seen walking through our landing and down towards their rooms. Emmet described him as the Cat-Faced Leader and explained that there was a group of beasts that followed him. This being had a cat-like face with two horns and snakes on its head, a horn on its nose, snake-like arms, and big wings with claws. Its tail had a rattle and it had "cobra things with skulls on them". It also had bird-like feet but as Emmet explained, "birds have three toes and he had four". It is this type of specific attention to detail that adds so much weight to their reporting. As you can see by the drawing, Emmet did not count the back talon as a toe at all which makes sense from a young child who is comparing the physicality of these beings to our own. So looking at bird feet in the same way, most birds have only three toes. According to Emmet, this entity was "evil" and led a group of demons that Emmet had observed on a few occasions, some of whom I have included below. The first two pictures are this Cat-Faced demon – the one on the left being the first time, and the one on the right being from a later sighting. The other pictures are examples of the "minions" who follow.

Cat-Faced Demon: Energy-Collector

To see a clearer copy go to www.aknowing.com or to the Facebook page: A Knowing- Living with Psychic Children

Cat-Faced Demon Entourage: Energy-Collectors

To see a clearer copy go to www.aknowing.com or to the Facebook page: A Knowing- Living with Psychic Children

The "Cat-Faced Demon" is an energy-collector type and may have been the source of the horrible smell that Emmet had picked up a few months earlier. The faces and skulls are symbolic of those that he has trapped. The same holds true for the extra heads on the dragon-like creature and the circular objects that adorn and surround the short chubby entity who are part of the entourage – they too are representative of trapped beings.

Similar Visions: Years Apart

This incident involving my daughter Anithe is interesting because, for me anyway, it validates that what these children are seeing are real. When Emmet saw the Cat-Faced Demon and its minions Anithe was only three years old. As she was asleep during the experience that Emmet shared with us she was not in any way privy to either the verbal or artistic details about the beings that Emmet had observed that night. While I collected any and all psychic comments and drawings that came through my children, I kept them tucked away from them, not wanting them to overly obsess or focus on these events, especially the negative ones. So Anithe had no prior knowledge of the incident of May 17, 2001.

In the summer of 2002, well over a year after Emmet had had his sightings, Anithe illustrated an entity that very much resembled the short chubby one with circles on and around him that Emmet had drawn as a follower of the Cat-Faced Demon. She described her drawing as *"the bad monster from my dream"*. Other than sharing that she was frightened by him she would not tell me anymore about him as she was trying to protect me. Because I rarely pulled out my "psychic file" to look at it, and did not remember the similar entity that Emmet had drawn, I did not make any connection when she handed it to me and explained what it was. It was Emmet who instantly recognized this entity the minute he saw the drawing and immediately drew my attention to the similarity. I waited until they had gone to bed before pulling out Emmet's drawing and comparing them. Emmet was right. Despite artistic and perceptual differences, they were obviously either the same or of the same type. I was not pleased.

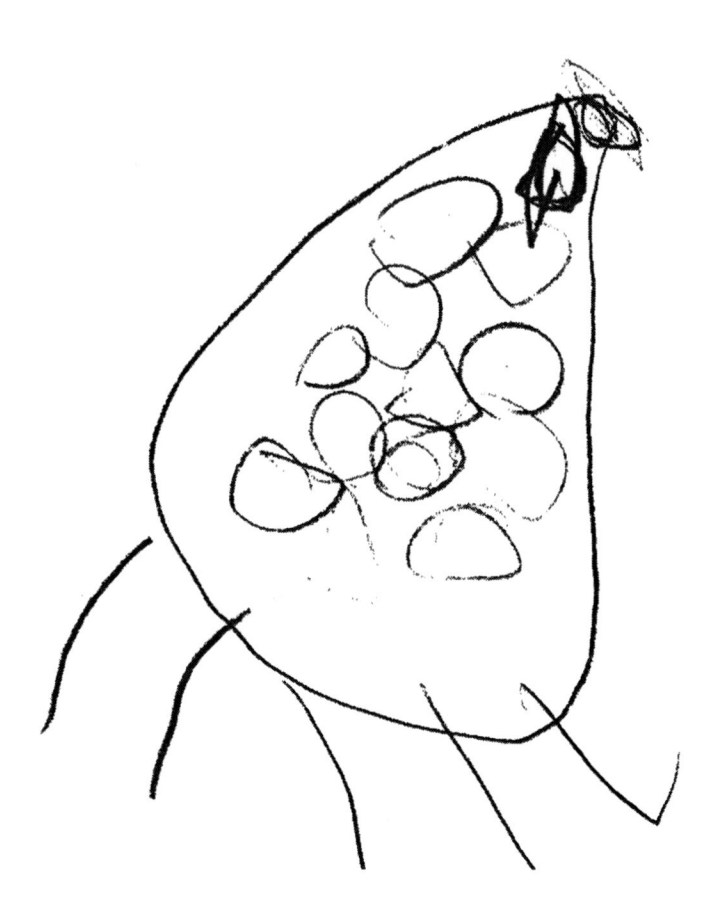

Energy Collector

To see a clearer copy go to www.aknowing.com or to the Facebook page: A Knowing-Living with Psychic Children

As my friend, John Collins, explained to me this particular being is of the same ilk as Emmet's but would be a more powerful or "senior" manifestation. His role however, is the same. He is an Energy-Collector (the circles on his body represent the many sources from which he draws energy) and beyond perpetuating his own existence and power by feeding off the energy of others, his job is to instill fear in all of us, especially the young children who posses psychic abilities and whose job is to counter negativity and low energy.

This was the only time that I am aware that Anithe saw this particular entity, and thankfully he never caused her any direct harm. I was sure to spend extra time with her over the next few days reminding her that I was there and she was loved and safe. It appears that this must have been enough for her to manifest the protection she required from this entity.

Another Energy-Collector

Anithe observed this Energy-Collector one day, and I found it particularly interesting because she perceived it in a different way than the others and so it makes for a good example of the type of variations that parents can watch for in their children's drawings. In the other instances where both she and Emmet had seen Energy-Collectors they had appeared with added appendages, extra heads, or circular objects attached to their bodies or under their cloaks that represented the individuals they had trapped. In this situation the individuals were circling the Energy-Collector. They appear to be free and unattached but they are not, and in fact if you look carefully you can see that they are within the energy field, or aura, of the collector.

Energy-Collector

To see a clearer copy go to www.aknowing.com or to the Facebook page: A Knowing-Living with Psychic Children

Anithe was very specific and consistent in the way that she drew these trapped beings. There are six above the being and six below it. The ones on the top all have three vertical lines and two horizontal ones. The ones on the bottom, which very much resemble the circles of light that some people refer to as "spirit orbs" that can be captured on film, especially digital cameras, all have a rectangle with lines like bars, and above these rectangles are round objects. However they appear children should not interact with these beings and efforts should be made to remove them if they are showing up persistently in a child's art or if they are interacting or communicating with them in any way.

Dead Men Walking

One of the most frightening and traumatizing types of experiences for sensitive children is observing human violence or the results of this type of negative action on a psychic level. This is partly because these are actions that occur around us every day in "real time" being committed by humans and so they can relate to them in a more tangible way. Monsters and distorted humans (that children usually do not identify as people) can be frightening enough, but to witness the negative actions of a human individual or individuals and not to be able to help in any way is very painful for these children even if it is an event that happened in the past.

Such was the case in 2005 when Connor was eleven years old and we went on a long weekend to the west of Ireland. We were all really enjoying ourselves, especially the kids, as there was water, seals and dolphins – a winning combination for them. We arrived at a certain location that was particularly bucolic and peaceful. Connor was obviously uncomfortable and stayed close to me throughout our meanderings there until suddenly he turned white, gripped my arm extremely hard and insisted that we had to leave immediately because he was "very afraid" and he "did not like this place". He seemed afraid to give too many specifics immediately but did refer to the fact that he had seen a man and little children and that something terrible had happened. As there was nobody at this spot but us, I knew it was a purely psychic experience. When we returned to our rooms, I approached him to discuss what he had witnessed but he was adamant that he was not going to talk about it. He was just too upset and frightened and did not want to revisit it. I reminded him that I was here for him and let the matter drop.

Three years later in 2008, my husband was in our room surfing the net looking for a house to rent for two weeks during the summer. I was reading next to him in bed and Connor was two rooms away, wearing headphones and watching a DVD on his computer. The other two were romping around, as usual. My husband found a house he thought had potential and mentioned the name of the town that it was in. The name sounded somewhat familiar but meant nothing to me and I continued reading after agreeing that the house was nice and the price was very reasonable. We were considering booking it. About fifteen minutes later Connor came into our room and asked if he could talk to me. I followed him to his room where he told me that a few minutes before he started remembering the vacation where he had become frightened. He could not understand why this had come into his head because he had not thought about the incident since it had happened. Then a possible connection hit me. I ran into our room and asked my husband if this house that he was considering was in the same town as the one where Connor had had this negative experience. As my husband did not remember the incident itself I had to describe the place we had stayed and he was then able to confirm that it was, in fact, the same place. This illustrates the sensitivity of these children. Three years after the incident, the minute his father had focused in on the energy of this town – on the specific energy of that area – by concentrating on the house and the local amenities, Connor had picked up on that energy and the experience and memories came flooding back to him. Neither Connor nor I remembered the name of the town, and while my husband knew the town's name and that we had stayed there, he did not immediately associate it with Connor's negative experience. And yet within minutes of my husband concentrating on this area, Connor was aware of that specific energy, knew what that energy meant, and became upset. The vivid detail that came through him when he finally shared was unbelievable. He even surprised himself. This is what he described,

"There were three children by the water…a pond - two boys and one girl. Their ages were between ten and twelve. The girl had brown wavy hair, a fancy white dress and white shoes. One boy was wearing a dark blue shirt and pants, while the other was dressed like him but in light blue. They both wore black shoes with golden buckles and they both had brown hair. There were about ten soldiers there. They were dressed in red long sleeved shirts, breastplates and helmets (we looked through a book later and he identified the roundhead type of helmets to be the ones that the soldiers wore). They had red pants and wore black boots. There was this man…I think he knew the children or may have been related to them. He was wearing a black shirt with poufy shoulders, black pants, a white frilly collar, a floppy black hat with a white feather in it, and black shoes with a golden buckle. He killed them. He drowned them one by one and I think he did it for power…to get them out of the way so he could have more power. It was awful…really, really awful." -C

Now it took a lot of coaxing to get him to finally open up about this as he sat pale and upset on his bed. He was under the impression that talking about it would somehow make it worse. But once he chose to share and the details came tumbling from his mouth, he felt great relief and was finally able to let go of it. Again, these children think they are protecting us, and so they can witness terrible events and beings and choose not to share them with us. It is important that they do. They must share and cleanse, not retain and repress. They must trust and know that only through communication can we ever attempt to help them – to give them guidance, support and protection (if that is what is required). So never give up, keep reaching out to them, even if it takes years. It is well worth it in the end when they can respond, share, and release.

Figure Walking Through House

On March 1st, 2004, when our family was sitting in the living room together, Anithe jumped, as if surprised by something, and said that she had seen a dark figure pass from one side of the room to the other, appearing from one wall and passing through another. I asked her to draw what she had seen, and explained to her that she had nothing to fear. I explained to her that we share space with many things that we don't usually see and that we don't really understand but that she should not be afraid, she should merely tell me what she sees, if and when she should see something.

Shadow Figure

To see a clearer copy go to www.aknowing.com or to the Facebook page: A Knowing-Living with Psychic Children

As it happened, this entity was just passing through and was not interested in interacting with us on any level that I am aware of. There is so much activity occurring around us, and most of it goes unnoticed by us. These children are open to it, which can be both a wonderful gift and a terrible burden depending on how much support these children feel they have and the environment that they find themselves in. As parents, we should also try to remember that the people who surround and interact with our children also define whether their gifts "torment" them or raise them up. Psychic children are very open to our emotional states and our thoughts, which they experience on a psychic and spiritual level, and this can be very frightening especially if negativity is emanating from an individual with whom they should feel safe. Often when there has been tension within a home or there is conflict between parents or a parent and child, these children will draw pictures of how they perceive these things on the psychic plane, but they will be usually unwilling to explain or discuss them. Other children will merely withdraw until these energies are cleared by the individuals themselves or by the child psychically cleansing their space. This ability adds an entirely different dimension to parenting and it can be overwhelming at times. All I can advise is open communication and dialogue; love and affection and lots of it; turn your back on fear and trust, trust, trust; and sit back and watch while they not only raise themselves up, they raise you up to unimagined levels along with them.

Chapter 6

Greater Insights

Psychic children have the ability and the habit of sharing great truths and insight without breaking a sweat. Sometimes these statements are hard to understand immediately or their significance is lost on the adult with whom they share. This is why it is important to keep track of whatever they communicate. It allows us to look back and understand the depth of what they have tried to teach us once we finally catch up with them. Other times these children will leave you speechless as they effortlessly, and using simple language and imagery, explain deep and difficult concepts with ease. It is never boring to be a parent of one of these children! This chapter covers many of these types of experiences that I had with my children.

My Other Mother

In January 2000, during a conversation regarding our family rules and the fact that they apply equally to all of us, Emmet informed me that he was "different". At first I found this to be a very amusing and clever way for a child to avoid having to keep in step with the rest of us, but as the conversation continued I realized that there was more depth to what he was saying. He spoke in a very matter-of-fact voice during our talk.

"Emmet, rules are rules and bedtime is bedtime. The rules apply to all of us."
–CP

"Not to me…I'm different." –E

"Oh really? How so?" –CP

"I'm different. My **other** mother told me that I am different." –E

"Your **other** mother?" –CP

"Yes. She's not from here, she is from somewhere else. She's not a person like you, she looks different." –E

"And she told you that you are different?" –CP

"Yes, I'm different. I'm not the same." –E

    I did not challenge him. Rather than argue with him over his statement, I accepted that he was different but explained that as he had decided to come here to Earth he had to follow some of our rules, at least until he was a little older. I explained that it wouldn't be fair if he ran riot while the other two did as they were asked. He considered this for a few seconds and then nodded as if he had come to a decision that what I had explained was acceptable to him. Before settling down to sleep he asked me if there was a word to describe someone who did not live here. I hesitated, because I did not want to define this being, this other mother, for him. Eventually I said the only word I could come up with was "alien" because it was a word that meant that someone or something was not originally from a certain place. I did also say that I may be wrong in defining her that way as I did not completely understand who or what she was. He seemed settled once he had an answer and went to sleep. He never mentioned this "other mother" again.

Many children, more now than ever, share this feeling that they are somehow different and are not from here. For some this is an indication that it may be their first sojourn here on Earth, while for others it is that they seem to retain an awareness that is often accompanied by a strong feeling that this is not their true home. While on one level they do not perceive the distinct separation between ourselves and the "All", they still seem to recognize that they are somehow separated from their True Source and that Earth is neither their place of origin nor their permanent residence. Sometimes they feel they are here through error, and this feeling may indicate that they (at least at that moment in time) think that their choice to come down to such a dense, low vibrating and emotionally charged atmosphere was a mistake on their part. Most of them adjust, but as their awareness begins to focus fully on this experience and they disconnect or power-down their ability to see beyond the veil, they sometimes experience panic or feel a sense of regret. They should not be belittled in any way if they share these thoughts and feelings as they need support and reassurance above all. Love eases them through their transition as well as helps them to accept where they are and the decisions that led them to be here. Having said that, they do need to understand that being different does not get them out of bedtime or any other *reasonable* rules or restrictions! Parents can certainly pursue this line of questioning more than I did. I was just too ignorant and surprised at the time to delve any further into it and, quite honestly, too eager for them to settle down to sleep so that I could do the same. I still wish that I had asked Emmet to describe this other mother in more detail as well as the place she lived so as to have been better able to discern what or who she was, but I was caught off guard. So if your child makes an unusual statement with conviction, don your Sherlock Holmes hat and start asking questions. You may be amazed at what they will share with you if they are willing and able.

When You Die You Still Live

It is important to try to listen to children when they are talking to you, but it is also important and enlightening to listen to them when they talk to each other as they often reveal jewels of wisdom when they communicate amongst themselves. On July 14, 2002 I heard Emmet speaking to his brother who had expressed a fear of death. Emmet, who was only six years old, was so pragmatic as he explained that there was no reason to fear death that it even took me by surprise. They were not aware that I was listening to them. Emmet explained,

*"You have to die to go back to be with God again. I don't believe that you can only live once…only one time. I think you can be human more than once. Anyway, you don't have to worry because **when you die, you still live**."*

What a beautiful and deep concept! Many of these children understand without being taught that death is not the end, and they are here to teach and reassure others – both peers and adults – that this is indeed the case. Sometimes they have opinions about the nature of our being that can be in conflict with the beliefs of others that surround them and the social group that they are in. These opinions should be respected because they represent the child's innate inner knowing. They should be respected, considered, approached and discussed with an open mind. In this case, reincarnation had not been discussed in our home and was certainly not communicated to Emmet through other conventional means. In terms of his wider environment, he was exclusively surrounded by people who considered themselves Agnostic or Christians, and neither recognizes reincarnation. He just knew within himself that this idea of multiple incarnations was true and that death represents a return to our origins and continued life. As I was not supposed to be privy to this conversation, I never made a comment about it to either Emmet or his brother. But it had a great impact on me. Slowly but surely these children will challenge us to open our minds, reexamine our thoughts and beliefs, and research, learn and grow.

More Than One Chance

The idea of reincarnation came up again later on and illustrates how, at least initially, children will cling on to their knowing and not immediately accept teachings or beliefs that are being presented to them as being fact when they are in conflict with their own. In this case Emmet had been taught in school that we only have one chance at life – there is no reincarnation. This is because in Ireland, where they were in school at that time, they are taught catechism as part of the curriculum, even in the public schools. This, of course, led to many interesting discussions by the children whose "knowing" was in conflict with much of what they were being taught in school. It also was interesting to see how each of my children were affected by these teachings and how they approached integrating or rejecting them based on their individual personalities, how connected they were to their inner-self, and how pliable or defiant their personalities were. It also depended on how much they cared or how important their own inner beliefs were to them. My eldest child did not much care what people thought or taught and so did not put much energy into focusing on any questions that dealt with spirituality. For the most part he just ignored all the religious ideas that were being taught. My other two felt these things deeply and were affronted that they were being definitively taught "truths" that they intuitively believed to be wrong. All three of them came to their own conclusions at different times in their lives and this freedom to do so was supported by the fact that the rule in our home is that everyone's opinion is considered as valid as another's. No one is allowed to mock or chastise, and while we may not agree with one another we have to respect the right of everyone to develop their own sense of reality and belief system.

When Emmet came home from school that afternoon, he was dumbfounded. He explained what he had been taught in school and asked me what I believed. In response I merely asked him *what he thought* which is an important thing to do when you are dealing with these children. They already carry the answer within them. But they are being taught and told by figures of authority that what they know innately is wrong, and this causes internal conflict and confusion. They do not need to be told by their parents what is "right" or "true". What they need is to be given the opportunity to look within themselves and reconnect with their knowing and rediscover the vast understanding that they came to us with. Once they have done that all they require from their parents is support for their beliefs even if it is in conflict with the general beliefs held by the family. This is what Emmet said on that day when I asked him what he thought:

"Of course there's more than one chance…one chance would be silly! Some souls never come back to Earth…most do though. If a soul had a very hard time on Earth and suffered a lot, they might not want to come back, so they could choose to stay with God where there was love and they felt safe."

There is no one on Earth that I am aware of who knows all there is to know about our souls, their journey, and the greater questions of existence and life. There is no one that knows what is absolutely true or is absolutely incorrect in relation to the spiritual and metaphysical. We spend much of our time thinking, studying, discussing, and searching for the truth and the best we can ever really hope for is that we find explanations that ring true to us. No one can honestly say that children who express unprompted beliefs that are in conflict with what they are being taught are wrong, and so I would encourage any parent of a psychically connected child to support them and respect what they share and not feel threatened by conflicting beliefs. The insights that children receive or "know" are as valid as any that has been handed down through the centuries from others with whom we have no connection. The fact that a belief has been accepted and maintained over time in no way makes a belief more valid than one that may be new (even if it is only new to the parent) and, in fact, the truths that come from children come to us fresh, honest, and unaltered and unedited by others who may have held their own prejudices or agendas.

All Happening Now

While driving to school one dark and wet October morning in 2004, Emmet suddenly began to speak as he stared out of the window. I have found that trips in the car often put them into a mild trance state and, if they speak on these occasions, they often reveal remarkable thoughts.

"I think I understand about dimensions now. I think the world is dimensions. See the dinosaurs are still here on Earth and you could see them if you could get into the right dimension. It's all happening now at the same time."

Quantum Physics in the morning! Why not? I had read about this in books but always had a terrible time trying to think in this way as my mind naturally leaned towards linear time with a past, present, and future that are clearly defined and are separate. But for Emmet, in that moment, it was all clear and did not pose the same confusion for him that it did for me. Why he was thinking about this on that particular day at that time, I have no idea. There had been no discussion prior to that moment that would have prompted this statement that I could think of, but this is what these kids can do.

Angel, Devil, Vortex

This picture was drawn by Emmet and left aside. He did not draw attention to it in any way, and I came upon it while I was cleaning up the usual household mess. It is a powerful drawing.

Angel, Devil, Vortex

To see a clearer copy go to www.aknowing.com or to the Facebook page: A Knowing-Living with Psychic Children

The angel and the devil represent Good and Evil, Light and Dark, or Yin and Yang, depending on how you feel most comfortable referring to them. They are the two sides of the coin that are present on Earth and appear to exist throughout our Universe. They are balance. The vortex, or portal, is the projection from where all that we experience comes from, or where our reality enters into three-dimensional existence. So this is an overview of our dimensional reality that includes a hint as to the source from whence this program, or experience, comes from.

Seeing With Your Mind

This occurred in December 2005 when Anithe was six years old. She wrote a note to her father that I found and queried. The note said,

"What you believe is what you see. Your mind is your eyes. Your eyes are just something."

When I asked her to explain what she meant, she explained that we see with our minds and so we cannot easily see what we do not accept to be true. An adult would have said, "Your beliefs define your perception". What was amazing about this, beyond the fact that she could understand this at such a young age, was that this was a lesson or understanding that my husband required. What I have observed is that these children are able to naturally, and without cognitive awareness, identify and share a specific and almost tailor-made lesson with the person who needs it. They don't run around sharing truths with everyone randomly, and often will not share with those whom they do not trust or love. But they can, and do, zero in on an individual and deliver a message or lesson that is sorely needed at that time in the person's life. What they teach us and say to us can often be uncomfortable to hear because it challenges our mind-set and our beliefs. But as time passes I think that most people are affected positively and will recognize the value of the insights and lessons that these children have brought to them.

God's Name: No Right Way of Saying His Name

On March 2006 while driving in the car Anithe, who was eight years old, stated out of the blue,

"There's no right way of saying God's name because God is everywhere and is everything. Everyone's name is God's name and everything is God's name.

God gave a piece of himself to everyone, but He is so great He can regenerate himself. There is God in all of us."

All I could think when she said this was, "Wouldn't this world be a much better place if everyone felt this way?" She explained to me that because God made all living things that all of them are Him and He is them. There really is no division, the division occurs within our own perceptions. You do not need a specific name for God. God is too large and too vast to be restricted to one moniker. She explained that every time we see or name something, we are observing and speaking God's name because All-is-Him and He-is-All. We are God because the spark that is our True Selves is God. Nature is God for the same reason, as Nature's energy is God's energy. We are all one in different forms. We are all, at our core, different expressions of the same Source. So, according to my eight year old daughter, God resides in all of us and in everything, all we have to do is recognize it.

Anithe's Observations

In October 2007, as a hypnotherapist, psychotherapist and Reiki Master, and because of the experiences I had had through my children, I was asked to speak at The World Ghost Convention and to the Psychological Society at The University College Cork. These speaking engagements led to my being invited to be part of a panel at the UCC Student Center that was to discuss things of a psychic and metaphysical nature, as well as alternative methods of healing in an informal setting. It was an interesting evening, especially as we all came from different backgrounds and had varying viewpoints and perspectives. It was the first time I had met all but two of the panelists, and of those one I had only met briefly a few evenings prior and the other I had only spoken with on a few occasions. I did not know any of them well. Unbeknownst to me there was some tension among a few of the other panelists who knew each other and there was some serious negativity coming from at least one of them. My daughter was sitting in the front row and had a notebook and pencil, as well as her teddy bear (which goes nearly everywhere with her). During the panel, she began to draw what she was seeing and sensing. Afterwards she shared the many pictures that she had drawn, three of which I will show here. She drew a torc that she saw on my forehead that she explained was there for my protection - protection that I was not aware I required at the time- and she drew two negative entities that were associated or attached to a member of the panel. It was not until I later learned about the negative situation that existed that her pictures all fell into place.

Protective Torc

To see a clearer copy go to www.aknowing.com or to the Facebook page: A Knowing-Living with Psychic Children

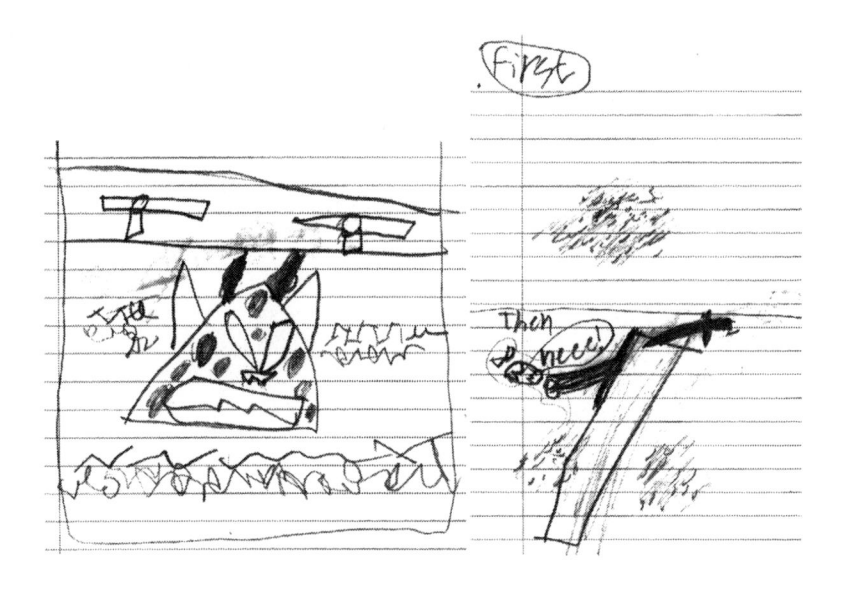

Negative Entities that Anithe observed

To see a clearer copy go to <u>www.aknowing.com</u> or to the Facebook page: A Knowing-Living with Psychic Children

The person who had attracted the entities had become involved in "black magic" and had drawn a lot of negative energy and entities to themselves. Anithe depicted the process and final result in the picture to the far right. "First" it began as negative energy and angry, dark feelings. But instead of allowing these feelings to dissipate, this individual fostered these feelings and "Then" gave them life through his own will and actions. The picture in the left, with the tell-tale circles on its face, is an energy-collector. This person is in a lot of trouble.

So children are more psychically aware than we give them credit for. If a child is uncomfortable around another person, it would be wise not to push them to interact with them. It is not necessarily that this person is "bad", but they may be giving off energy frequencies that the child is not able to handle or is uncomfortable with at that moment in time. Depression, sadness, anger, drugs, and alcohol are only a few examples of things that can change our frequency and the energy of a person and it can make some children quite uncomfortable. So as awkward as it may be at times, try to respect or at least don't discount children's reactions to others even if they can't (or won't) fully explain why they are uncomfortable around certain individuals.

"No" to Confirmation

In Ireland, children automatically began to receive Catechism once they enter the school system as it is part of the public school curriculum. These religious lessons provided many insightful and interesting discussions as my children questioned and often rejected outright what was being taught. Sometimes they were merely perplexed by what they were learning. I always felt that it was educational, not because catechism was teaching them about Christianity, but because it forced them to think and question their core "knowing" and to analyze their own beliefs. I was always careful not to influence them with my own opinions or share my thoughts until they had come to their own conclusions. So if one of them came home and said, "Today we were told…is that true?" I would respond, "What do you think?" and allow them to discuss and explore their own opinions before offering any of my ideas, if they were even still interested in what I had to say!

People may wonder why my husband and I chose to baptize our children into the Catholic faith considering the non-religious and fairly strong anti-institutional views that were held by both of us. There were many reasons. One was that we felt that they should be exposed to the religious heritage of their Christian family (Protestant, Catholic, Syrian Orthodox) and since they were Irish-American and Catholicism played so heavily in the history of the Irish, we chose Catholicism. As Catholicism was part of their Irish school curriculum it was a convenient way of exposing them to a religion and the idea of an institutionalized belief system. It also allowed them to explore this approach to spirituality so that they could decide themselves whether or not they wanted to accept this type of belief system or not. So, knowing that they could make up their minds as they developed and learned, and knowing that they would be exposed through both of us and by my side of the family to different ideas if they were interested, I felt comfortable that baptizing them as Catholics and exposing them to catechism through school was a good idea overall.

When Emmet entered 6th Class, which would be 7th Grade in America, he began to prepare for his Confirmation. His brother Connor had gone through it the year before, and almost all of his class was involved in the preparation for this Sacrament. Being a Catholic country there is great anticipation and excitement that surrounds these Sacraments, with parties and dinners and gifts, usually in the form of money. Very few children ever question whether or not Confirmation is something that they will do, as it is assumed that they will. One thing that I found very strange was that the concept that Confirmation is a choice, that this is the first opportunity these children have to actually make a decision about their spiritual future, is not communicated to them by the teachers, priests or even their family. I questioned friends of mine whose children were at different schools and none of them, parents or children, seemed to even be aware that "choice" was involved at all. The best illustration came from one of my dearest friends who, when I asked about the right to choose whether or not children wanted to do their Confirmation paused for a long time before stating in a very confused voice, "*Is* it a choice? I mean *can* you do that…not do your Confirmation?" So choosing not to do your Confirmation in Ireland, when you are considered to be a Catholic, is a rarity to say the least.

Approximately one week before Emmet's Confirmation, the evening before his Confession (which is done in school which was good as we never went to church), Emmet came to me and stated that he did not think that he wanted to do his Confirmation but he was not willing to tell me why. The most he would say was, "Well, who is this guy (the priest) anyway? He's not God. He can't forgive and absolve me, only God and I can do that. It's ridiculous!" I explained that this was part of the Catholic faith and it would be a part of his life if he wanted to continue to be a Catholic. I suggested that he question the priest about this issue and ask him any questions he may have and then see how he felt afterwards. He nodded and went to bed. As it turned out, he did not have the opportunity to speak to the priest as there were so many boys waiting in line that he did not feel it was the time to get into a deep discussion. So he let it go.

As the days counted down towards Confirmation, Emmet did not mention anything about it and so I decided to give him space and not to bring it up. Two nights before Confirmation he again came to me and announced that he had thought about it and that he definitely did not want to make his Confirmation and that he was now willing to explain why. He again referred to his objection to Confession through a priest, seeing him as more of an unnecessary obstacle. He did not agree with the idea and statement in the ceremony that they were "not worthy" of God and God's love, he had a tremendous problem with the idea that up to the point of Confirmation the Holy Spirit had not been with them and that a person (the priest) had the "power" and was necessary to call the Holy Spirit to anyone. In his mind, if there is a Holy Spirit it is ever-present and with everyone, and because God made us and is a part of the "real" us, there is no true separation between us and Him - we just think there is. He could not accept being separate or afraid of God and requiring all these people and ceremonies to somehow come closer to Him. In his mind, the Church sets the fear and reinforces the separation, and then it offers itself up as the bridge between people and God, only further cementing the sense of separation, fear and the need for priestly ambassadors and communicators. As his views and beliefs were so in conflict with Catholicism, he had made the very brave and mature decision that he could not, in good conscious, embrace Catholicism and become a member of the Church. "I still love Jesus though," was the final comment he made.

Before I say anymore, I would like to say that Emmet's Class Teacher and School Principle were wonderfully supportive when I went to speak to them at the eleventh hour about Emmet's decision and in the weeks that followed his decision. And aside from a few phone calls on the evening of the Confirmation from bewildered friends and some third-degree from classmates the next school day, almost everyone dealt with his choice very well. Emmet's choice was right for Emmet. The decision others make when committing to spiritual or religious beliefs is what is right for them, and so this part of the book should in no way be taken as a condemnation of Catholicism or their beliefs and rituals. The significance of this story is that psychic children have an extremely defined knowing that is linked to their core and they will try to communicate and defend it. Some will be willing and able to stand up to authority and respected institutions. They have come to affect change. They have come to challenge us individually and to help us take back the control and power we gave away to others. They are brave and they are confident. They are teachers and warriors, and make no mistake, unless we actively strip them of all self-esteem and confidence they will enlighten us, empower us, and change this world for the benefit of us all.

Mediation & A Personal "Religion"

About 18 months before my son Emmet decided not to do his confirmation, my daughter Anithe decided that she did not agree with what she was being taught in Catechism and, in fact, did not very much like most of what she was hearing. So at the age of 7 ½ she began to ask me to read things to her about different views and beliefs. Beyond holding her own very strong ideas she began asking about Buddhism and Taoism. Even with these religions she did not accept everything I outlined for her, which again shows how confident children can be in determining their beliefs if they are given the freedom to develop and express their inner-knowing. To be fair, I did not know much about these religions myself and did not spend much time explaining either of them to her, although we did look them up on Encarta.

Feeling very protective and loving of Jesus, she began by deciding she would be a Christian-Buddhist-Taoist. She felt that this would allow her to draw what she liked best from all three religions. After checking with me to be sure this was "alright", which I assured her it was, she happily settled in to this. Soon afterwards she asked me if she could make up her own spirituality based on what she thought was true and real. I told her that she could, and so again she was happy, coming to share her ideas and thoughts with me from time to time.

In March 2008, at the age of nine, while watching a movie, Anithe learned that to meditate you merely need to relax, clear your mind, and allow things to come to you. She promptly grabbed a pillow over which she placed an oriental rug, and disappeared into her room to try this "mediation". About an hour later she emerged to announce she had three ideas to share that had come to her while meditating. My husband, my best friend Siobhan, and I sat back silently expecting childish statements. She had written the ideas on a paper that she had illustrated beautifully with a picture of a being she said had communicated these ideas to her.

Sa-Ma(n)-Tha-Co(l)-Danas

To see this in color go to www.aknowing.com or to the Facebook page: A Knowing-Living with Psychic Children

The ideas or concepts she had received were: *"Why have materials, if materials is not a life?"*, *"If everything is everything, then what is individual?"*, and finally *"Needs are needs, but wants are distractions"*.

The first thing that struck me, besides the fact that these were amazing concepts and statements for any child to make, was the fact that there were grammatical errors. Anithe had perfect grammar and would rarely, if ever, make such obvious errors. It was almost as if she was translating for another, or another was translating to or through her. What also struck me was her understanding of the statements and concepts she had received.

The first, concerning materials, questions the emphasis we have placed on material gains and possession of material items and challenges us to consider how we value them in relation to life and living things. The second deals with the concept that We-Are-All-One and the fact that all living things are, in reality, connected both in this plane and beyond it. It questions and challenges us to consider that the separation we perceive between living things, or "everything" as she says, does not really exist. It also asks that we consider what it is that we believe to be the definition and the significance of being an individual or of having the opportunity to experience separateness and being an individual being. The third absolutely blew me away because it is so powerful and so true, and seems to outline one of the futile goals we strive for as a society and individually and that has contributed greatly to our feeling so miserable and empty – the continuous focus and desire for goods to define our success or to fill the empty void within us. Obviously living within this dense dimension, we require things to survive and to avoid suffering. This is not called into question. Anithe herself explained to me, "It doesn't mean the basic things like clothes and a place to live and stuff you need…just the other things that aren't necessary." But much of the things we desire are above and beyond that which we need. Our "wants", are mere distractions that keep our minds and attention focused away from what is real and important, from those very things that may in fact bring us true happiness, fulfillment and understanding. Our "wants" change from day-to-day as we acquire each new target on our list. Our target list grows in size and alters regularly as we are bombarded by new and improved things which we can attain, and as we allow ourselves to feel as if we "need" these items in order to feel happy and fulfilled, or to reward ourselves. We are looking to fill the void, but never succeeding because we are trying to fill it in the wrong way. We are aware enough to recognize the emptiness within but we are just misguided in how we attempt to deal with it.

The other aspect of these statements which amazed me was the fact that she so succinctly summarized concepts that would take so much longer for most people to explain. This is one type of "sign" that I have used when attempting to identify and then categorize these messages. In Emmet's scrolls that related to God ("God Made Jesus"), part of what made it so powerful was that he explained so much in so few words and that he expressed concepts that were far beyond his years. Normally all young children ramble on in their innocent and childlike manner, so pay particular attention to them when they share such huge ideas in such tight and succinct statements. This is when it is time to put down the phone, book, or newspaper and listen and remember what they say before they release it and run off to shove Play-Doh up their noses!

In terms of Anithe's contact during her meditation, I have no idea who this entity is that she illustrated and who communicated such beautiful and thought-provoking statements to her, but I appreciate very much that these insights were shared. Anithe referred to the entity as "Sa-Ma(n)-Tha-Co(l)-Dana(s)" and as you can see from the picture she appears to be a very colorful horse-headed goddess. I feel her "name" and dress are clues to her message and origin, but have not had luck in engaging anyone who could help me. For example, I found the sounds Brianna associated with this deity have meaning in the Tibetan language but I have not had luck in confirming that this is, indeed, Tibetan or how these words may change in meaning or nuance when they are combined with one other. According to the Nitartha International Online Dictionary, the meanings of the words Anithe spoke, looked up phonetically, mean:

Sa – Earth or Earth element

Ma – female goddess or mother

Tha – everything; all; total

Co(l) – head; view; slight; blame; reproach; gullible

Danas – from now on; now; at present; immediately

While I will continue to search to find the true meaning of these words and to try to discover who the entity is that communicated them to Anithe, I feel that finding those answers is not as important as considering the messages themselves and taking stock of how we view and approach our life, one another, and our environment.

As an aside, to date Anithe has never bothered to meditate again.

Our Reality, Our Experience

This is one of the most significant concepts that Emmet ever shared with me. It came from his desire to make a present for my office when I began my new practice in Hypnotherapy and Psychotherapy. The present he gave me was a picture that explained what Emmet defined as "our experience". This is the simplest, most accurate, and most straightforward description that I have ever read or heard regarding this topic.

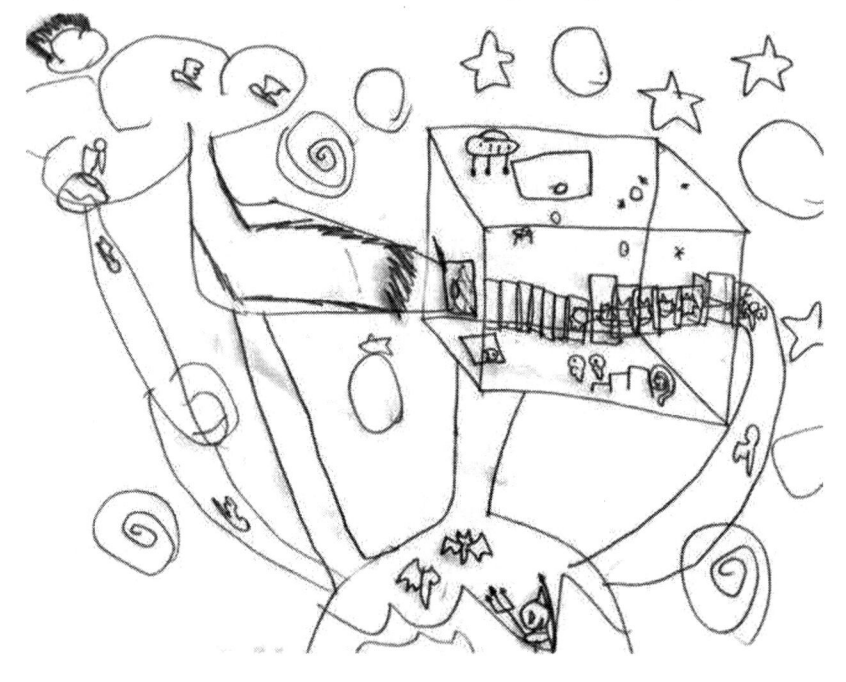

Our Experience

To see a clearer copy go to www.aknowing.com or to the Facebook page: A Knowing-Living with Psychic Children

"The souls come down and into the box that represents what we know. Each square within the box represents the passage of time, as well as multiple dimensions. Each square has millions of dimensions within it. The aliens, *who are not from our reality, can come into it when they want to or need to. If souls aren't ready to go back to Heaven after they die then they can stay as ghosts until they realize they are loved or they decide that it is time. If they don't believe they have been good they can also go to where the demon is. But they can return to the Light anytime they want to. They only don't when they don't think God loves them or when they don't think they deserve God's love. That's the problem with demons and things…they cause so much trouble because they are angry because they think that God doesn't love them. When a soul goes back to God, back to the Light, they are really happy and get stronger. Then, if they want to experience an event, or if they didn't accomplish their mission they can come back again."*

Most of this description is self-explanatory; however I would like to clarify what he said about the squares that represent the passage of time and the millions of dimensions within each square. This may seem ridiculous, but we must remember that every time we come to a cross-road, every time we are faced with a major decision, the option we do not take is also played out in another dimension/reality. We have, therefore, created millions of alternative dimensions/reality without ever being aware of it on top of the dimensions that exist independently of us. Emmet, and many other children like him, *are* aware of this fact. They know it without understanding why or being overwhelmed by these concepts.

The other thing that is so significant about this explanation is that as a child he understands that we define our own reality, our own experiences both here and in our spirit state. **We** are the only ones who have the ability to lock ourselves away from God's love. No one does this to us. If we believe that we are unworthy of God's love then that is the reality we will manifest for ourselves both here and after death. There is no punishment involved. No judgment by others. Only we judge ourselves and we manifest our own punishments and situations when we cannot forgive ourselves or others. Even the demons, as he calls them, are merely as they are because they have forgotten that they are loved or believe themselves unworthy of love. This may seem an amazing and impossible truth because we have been taught since we were young that demons were evil and dark, Satan being the worst of all. But remember that all that has ever been created is of God because He is Creation and provides the spark of energy that everything needs in order to exist and have life. Satan himself was once Lucifer, the brightest shining angel in Heaven. His emotion and thought became distorted and he allowed it to perpetuate and even cultivated it. As this cycle continued his God-Light became obscured from him. It became hidden so that he no longer could see or feel his beautiful perfection. This emptiness, this sense of separation from God and being filled with darkness fuelled other distorted thoughts and emotions such as anger and revenge which, in turn, distorted his form. God allowed this because of love and free will – He has allowed Lucifer to choose his own path. Lucifer, now Satan, has sentenced himself to his dark and hate-filled prison because he cannot see that deep within him the Light of God still shines, waiting to be recognized. He cannot see that he is still loved and that he merely needs to forgive himself and seek forgiveness and love from those he has rejected, especially his Maker. He needs to remember his origins and recognize the precious value of the Light that still exists within him. But will he? Will we? We are not so different from Lucifer, and his story makes for a good metaphor for the arrogance and blindness of the human race. We came from the same Source of Light and we are all meant to return to It. So we come from Love and can return to Love if we deem ourselves worthy…the choice is ours.

This whole concept of good and evil and the "reality" of our experience in the Third Dimension was something that confused me quite a bit. People would often say that evil did not exist or that what we were experiencing here was not "real" somehow. I would look around me and see acts of cruelty or apathy that I would consider evil. I would see great suffering and great joy and love feel that it was all pretty real. So when people would say, "don't worry about it, evil doesn't really exist," or "this isn't really happening anyway," I could accept it on a theoretical level but I could not get my head around it on a practical one, which caused me a good bit of confusion and conflict. For those of you who also have had difficulty understanding or coming to terms with this concept I offer this simple theory and explanation.

There is an ultimate point of True Reality, or True Existence, which is what we often refer to as God or the Source. And there, in this "place" of being, neither evil nor good exist because there is no emotion. It is a state that is beyond emotion. It is the purest form of being or of existence. I AM. I EXIST. But within our "experience" we accept, create, and perpetuate the emotions of good/love and evil/fear. We cannot imagine life or a consciousness existing without them and so we cause them to exist and they feel real to us. Our consciousness has chosen, or has been sent, to create and participate in this reality. We have chosen to immerse ourselves in this experience and so it is, for the time being, very real regardless of the ultimate point of True Reality.

In order to understand this we must understand that True Existence is not "good" or "evil", it just "Is". And the energy of what "Is" permeates and animates everything. We take this energy and we choose what to do with it. So *we* create dark and light, *we* create good and evil. In our reality, in our dimension and in many others, these things do exist but in terms of the ultimate point of True Existence neither exists – only existence exists – It just Is. When we use the energy from the Source in a positive way, we don't feel any fear. Fear seems to be the cause of what we call "evil". Those who take the energy and use it negatively begin to use it negatively out of fear and then that very same fear not only perpetuates their negative behavior and manifestations but also prevents them from returning to the Source, to True Existence. This self-imposed separation from the Source is what we refer to as Hell. It's very important to understand this because we fear what we call evil but at the point of True Existence it does not exist and therefore has no power or effect on our True Selves, our Inner Light, our God-Spark, our Soul. But if evil does not really exist, and good does not really exist, and this experience is not "real", why bother? Why make the effort to be "good"? We come here to learn, among other things, how to use the energy of the Source in the most effective and most efficient way and the closest thing we have to using and expressing this energy in a perfect manner is Love. So we must strive to express Love in all that we do and to create from a position of Love at all times. This is a great challenge in such a dense dimension but we accepted this challenge by coming here and we must rise to it as best we can in hopes that we can succeed.

Evil is something that we must take responsibility for as a collective life form or as a species. We are creative beings. The Source gives and we create. We must try our hardest to create positive experiences for ourselves and for others and to understand that, in the end, there is nothing to fear. To raise ourselves up we must learn to release the fear that others have passed onto us over the years as well as learn to deflect the fear others wish to draw us into and immerse our consciousness in. This is a difficult concept to understand and an even more difficult lesson to put into practice. I think that because of this there are many levels of learning and of growing, some physical and some less so, that allow us to gain more insight, experience, and perspective and allows us the opportunity to learn to use the energy properly until we are able to fully merge our consciousness, our Inner Light, with the True Existence that is God.

Chapter 7

Helpful Hints

The bad dreams and the sighting and sensing of negative entities began about two months after Emmet had told me about his symbolic dream of being in "Jesus' tummy". By March 10, 2000 he had become so terrified that he would not go anywhere alone and would cry and shake at bedtime. He was so fearful of what he would see and experience at night that he would often go to sleep in my arms claiming that he would not allow himself to sleep. This was an extremely traumatic time for him. Speaking to his doctor, the term "night terrors" was mentioned, which is a term that is used to describe something that the medical profession don't really understand. I knew this was a misdiagnosis.

Usually, with night terrors, the child does not recognize their parents and will appear confused. This was never the case for Emmet. He was always very cognizant when he awoke no matter how upset he was. He was able to recognize me, demonstrated no disorientation in terms of his location, and could describe and even draw what he had seen or experienced in great detail. When I further explained to our pediatrician that he also experienced these things during the day when he was awake, this was explained away as an "over-active imagination". Neither of these explanations fit, but to be fair to our doctor, who was really very good, he was merely attempting to define my problems within the restricted parameters of what he knew. He was hardly going to tell me that my child was psychic and was experiencing paranormal and psychic activity!

I then turned to psychics to try to get some helpful advice. It is really important, no matter what type of advice you are seeking, that you find someone who you trust – whether they are traditional advisors, like a priest or doctor, or a non-mainstream one, like a psychic. Some of the advice I got was neither practical nor helpful, such as washing down all the floors and walls with ammonia (hardly feasible in a 3,000 sq ft house that included carpeted areas). Needless to say I did not follow much of this – and this is the crux of what I am getting to. Have confidence in your own "knowing". No matter who is advising you, listen to your inner voice, your "gut" feeling, because it is usually right. If you feel that the advice you are getting is either worthless, misguided, or does not feel right for you, do not follow it. I have had the experience of both being given useless information, as well as having the honor of meeting extremely kind and experienced psychics and healers who shared freely of their time, knowledge, insight, understanding and advice. It took me a while to find them, and in fact they only came into my life when I was ready for them and, ironically, when I had stopped looking in a panic (fear) and had begun to trust (love), learn, and develop my own understanding through my children and research (taking responsibility) of how vast all possibilities are. There is no point in the Universe giving you the answers if you are neither willing nor able to accept or understand them. To all of these wonderful individuals, to the psychics and healers who were there for me when I was ready, I will be forever grateful for their insight, guidance and generosity of spirit.

As for your own quest for answers, continue the search both internally and externally and invite your child to ask for their own help from the Light while sitting in a state Of-Love. You know your child better than anyone else. You are the one who is caring for them and experiencing these events with them, so you are really the only one who knows if any advice or diagnosis is correct or not. I know it is hard, but be strong, be brave, and don't allow yourself to be led around because, in the end, you are the guardian of these children, if only for a little while until they can navigate this world on their own.

A Bit of Advice

The purpose of my book is to highlight the real phenomenon of the psychic awareness of children, and to give examples of some of the things that they and their parents may encounter and have to deal with because of their child's openness and abilities. Not having anyone else's experiences to reassure me, or explanations of what may have been going on with my children contributed greatly to my anxiety, doubt, and fear as my children shared their psychic experiences with me. I do hope that parents of psychic children who are reading this can take solace in the knowledge that they are not alone, that they are not crazy in thinking that what their child is experiencing is both psychic and real, and that they can release all fear in order to better understand these events and feel empowered to help and support their child.

Remember that the power to accomplish all things comes from within. It is the power of Love and of Light that is our Essence. When we combine this Love (Emotional-Energy) and Light (Source-Energy) with Intent and Belief (Thought-Energy), there is nothing that we cannot accomplish. Anything else, whether it is a tangible object such as a crystal, or a ceremonial practice or a prayer are merely vehicles that we use to help us focus our power, energy, and intent. These things act as helpful crutches to allow us to accomplish that which we can already achieve spontaneously. There is absolutely nothing wrong with using aids, but we must recognize that these objects and rituals do not hold any power in and of themselves. We are the ones who bestow power upon them. An analogy of this might be an electrical socket. This socket is energy waiting to be tapped, waiting to be channeled and utilized as needs require. It is what you plug into the socket that determines how that energy will be focused and used, and to what purpose. We have all the energy and power we need, we merely need to figure out how to focus and use it. This applies to mundane, everyday tasks as much as to spiritual ones. It applies whether we use only our minds to focus our energy or whether we combine it with objects or rituals. We can accomplish things by ourselves, we just often don't realize it and have not been trained to approach things in this manner. Having said that, there are times when we all feel that we need support, added expertise, or perhaps an item or "ritual" that will help guard or protect our children and our home, or clear low or negative energy from around us as I did when I bought rosary beads or had the house blessed. If it helps to dissipate fear and supports a feeling of safety and protection then, by all means, do it. The better you feel the higher your vibration will be; you will attract higher vibrating energy and entities to you; and you will create a "natural" protection for yourself, your family, and your environment. I just want to emphasize that these items and rituals are powerless in and of themselves. Their effectiveness comes purely from the energy we give over to them and the power we afford them.

"What do I do; where do I turn; who can I trust?" were the questions that haunted me the most. I do not pretend to have all the answers but I will share some of the things that I have tried myself. I hope readers will find this helpful. If you feel that you need to share a story or require further guidance or advice than what I have provided here, then please feel free to look at my website www.aknowing.com or on my Facebook page *A Knowing - Living with Psychic Children* and I will reply as soon as possible.

Before dealing with some simple suggestions on clearing or protecting someone from negative energies and entities, I would like to emphasize that you should look at your family situation and relationships first. Is there any animosity or tension within the family unit? In unhappy, tense, or confrontational environments we emit low and negative energy. We create our own areas of dense, dark matter that in turn attracts like energy and entities. Trying to protect a psychic child or clear negative energy from a house where there is deep seeded resentment or tension is an uphill battle that will not be easily won. Consider your thought patterns and the patterns of thought, words, and behaviors of other family members. Thought, word and deed are great creators, so be careful what creations you are giving life to! The question is, are you and your family creating and attracting positive energy and entities or negative ones? Whatever your answer may be, please take a few minutes to consider the state of the family before spending too much time, energy, and money attempting to place your finger in the proverbial dyke. Having said this, any forward motion is positive and represents a desire and commitment to affect change. So if you find that you are unable to tackle the larger issues, do not despair. Begin with smaller steps like clearing the house and holding the intention that this clearing positively touches everyone in the house. By beginning with the smaller steps, the larger issues may sort themselves out.

Another thing to pay attention to is when a psychic child describes a dream. Because we have been exposed to psychological or clinical dream analysis, we tend to see dreams as purely products of the mind and rarely of something greater or external. Sometimes this is indeed the case, and sometimes it is not. There are times when the dreams these children have are of great significance and should not be overlooked or underestimated in terms of their spiritual value. The other reason parents should listen when psychic children speak of dreams is that *sometimes they are not dreams at all*; indeed the child may be describing an entity, scene, or an object that they have seen with their waking eyes. Because these children recognize that there is some sort of difference between that which exists in our Third Dimension and what exists in others, and because their vocabulary is limited in terms of explaining what they are observing, they can present or describe psychic events that they experience while they are awake as "dreams". In their minds, because what they are seeing is not part of this Third Dimensional "reality" it must be classified as a dream. Simply ask them if they were asleep or awake when they had their "dream" or when this "dream" occurred. Their responses will always be immediate and practical, and understanding the nature of their experience will help you to discern between them and better understand what is occurring with your child.

Love, Intent, Belief, but No Fear

At the risk of being repetitive, love, intent, and belief are the three most effective tools you have when dealing with psychic issues - when listening and considering what your child has shared with you and when employing any "strategy" for protection and cleansing. You must sit in a state Of-Love so that your energy is at its optimum level, allowing you to access your innate strength, inner power, and knowing. Your intent and belief in what you are doing are extremely important if your efforts are to be as effective as possible. There is no point in being wishy-washy or approaching things with the attitude of, "I hope this works," or "I think this may have an effect". Do it or don't. If you approach anything with disbelief or doubt then the Universe will respond in kind. Your efforts will be rewarded in the same wishy-washy, tentative way in which you approached them. And finally, discard your fear. Fear has no use whatsoever, except perhaps to make you completely ineffectual and handicapped in any efforts you may make or work you do. At its best fear may merely serve as an excuse to do nothing, causing you and your child to stagnate instead of grow, locking you in a prison of your own making – something that I experienced first-hand albeit only for a short period. Know without doubt that you and your child are loved and protected and that the Universe and Light are there to help and support you. Know and believe it with every fiber of your being. Then set your intent and move forward.

Psychic Shield

Psychic shields can help protect a sensitive child and are no harm for anyone, psychic or not, to employ. They are simple to set up and easy to maintain. Try to set a calming tone in the room with soft lighting and music and whatever else you feel will help you and your child to relax. Ask them to get in a comfortable position and using a peaceful voice, talk them through a short guided relaxation of no more than a few minutes. Speak in a calm and soothing voice, and take your time in saying the words and going from one sentence or suggestion to the next. You are trying to lull them into a state of peace and relaxation. You could begin it as follows:

"Now that your eyes are closed you can feel your whole body relaxing…all your muscles relaxing…take a deep breath and blow it out and as you do you become even more relaxed…good job…let's try it again…in…out…relax… you are like a rag doll…you feel warm and safe and you know that you are loved."

Have them picture a place they love to be or doing something that makes them feel happy and safe. This is just to engage and kick-start their imaginations so they are ready to construct their psychic shield. For example:

"Imagine yourself in your hide-out with teddy… it is a sunny day and you have brought some of your favorite things with you…what did you bring?

(get them to describe a few things)…are you happy there?…wonderful…can you hear any sounds? (let them describe)…can you smell anything? (again, let them describe)…how do you feel?…excellent…you are very happy and safe in your hide-out, aren't you?"

Don't get upset or insist that they must see, hear or feel anything if they say that they can't. It makes no difference. You can just ask them to go to a happy place and let them describe it to you before moving on, without ever prompting or questioning them at all. Again, it is just to give them time to relax and engage their imaginations. Don't spend too much time doing this as children enter a relaxed state very quickly and easily and you don't want them falling asleep on you!! As they begin to relax, they will become more and more quiet and introspective as they give way to their own inner space and visions.

Once the child is relaxed, ask them to imagine that they can see, within themselves, a bright white light that shimmers like shiny white-silver. This light is shaped like a ball that shines or glows brightly and is located in the center of their chest or torso.

"I want you to imagine that there is a ball of silvery-white light glowing and shining in the center of your chest. (pause) Can you see it? Is it nice? Do you like it? Good."

From there they need to enlarge the light so that it encompasses their entire body, so that their whole body is glowing and shining with this amazing white-silvery light. Once they can imagine this, ask them to visualize the light forming a skin-tight body suit around them. The image you are going for here is a bit like the Silver Surfer from the Fantastic Four. It helps if you describe this final image or even have them draw a picture of what it will look like before you start this process so there is no confusion during it.

"You're doing really, really well. You have an amazing imagination! Now you need to make the light grow bigger and bigger so it is as big as you…so that it goes all the way out to your skin. Let me know when you have done that, ok? (Wait) Already??? Wow, you are really good at this! Remember how we talked about the silver suit? Good. Let's see if you can make the light form that suit on your body, just like the Silver Surfer! Tell me when you have done that too."

Guide them to ensure that this shield remains in place through their intention and that it serves as a protection for them – they can think these intentions or say them out loud.

"This shield protects me and nothing can penetrate/get through it unless I let it/want it to/I give permission. It cannot be broken. I am completely safe."

Once your child has completed constructing their shield and have opened their eyes, you can tell them that they are now a super-hero! Be sure that your child checks their shield on a regular basis based on their requirements or needs. For example, a child who is experiencing regular negative episodes should check their shield every morning and every night, while a child that does not seem as predisposed to negative experiences can check it once a month. My children check it every morning before going to school. To check their shields all they need to do is close their eyes and view their shields from the outside, or by using an imaginary mirror that they can imagine in their minds. Tell them that if there is an area of the shield that is dented, scratched, or that has disappeared, they merely need to visualize it as fixed and intend it to remain that way. This takes no more than a few seconds and it both protects and empowers. While I know that some psychics have multiple layers to their shields that are made of different shapes, colors, textures and materials, I feel that for most children this basic but all-encompassing protection should suffice. However, should your child want to visualize a different color for their shields then respect their choice as this is coming from their inner knowing and they are being guided to that color for a reason. Perhaps it is a color vibration that they specifically require at this time that will be more effective and provide more protection than the silver-white I am suggesting here. Again, be flexible and go with what is right for your child.

If your child is too young to manage these visualizations do not be concerned as there are two other alternatives: you can get them to merely state the intention that they are protected, *"I have a shield (and angels) around me that protect(s) me always."*, or you can construct a shield for them. Constructing a shield for your young child is not contrary to Universal Law as it does not impinge upon their free will as they are still your ward and you are doing it for their highest good. Do encourage them to construct their own shields as soon as they are old enough though as this empowers them and helps them to understand that they are capable of requesting and creating the protection and help that they need on their own.

Pyramid of Light

This is an extremely powerful and effective technique for protection. You can visualize a pyramid of pure, white light around anyone or anything - your child, your house, or your car. Children should be guided to close their eyes and to see themselves completely encased within this pyramid of white light. Be sure that it even forms a floor under their feet. Then give them the affirmation that their pyramid of white light (or the color of their choosing) will remain around them and protect them. You can follow the basic sequence of the Psychic Shield script. Be sure to reinforce that they are completely safe and that nothing can penetrate this pyramid of light without their consent. Repeat this as needed, or at night before they fall asleep. Again, you can construct these pyramids for them. Whenever my children go out I place pyramids around them, any vehicle they may be travelling in, or buildings they may be spending time in.

Visualizations

Visualizations are excellent and very powerful. When visualizing, approach it as if the healing, protection, or whatever it is you are hoping to accomplish is already achieved. State it in your mind or see it as an established fact. This certainty lends tremendous power to your efforts. After making yourself comfortable and reaching a relaxed state, picture your child standing in front of you. Then completely surround them with light and hold the intention that they are safe, protected, healed, etc. You can visualize as many layers of light as you want, placing each one over the next and sealing the light with your intention for each. You can give them different shapes and textures; combine them in a marbleized fashion; or work and manipulate them in any other way that you wish. The energy patterns for basic colors are as follows:

BLUE = protection and sealing in
GREEN = healing
RED = will power and passion
YELLOW = courage
ORANGE = vitality, ambition, and balance
INDIGO = psychic awareness
VIOLET = spiritual connection
WHITE = all prime color energies combined and is strong for protection and purity
PINK = unconditional love
GOLD = love and peace, or Christ energy

Do these visualizations as often as you want to or whenever feel there is a need. Always remember that everything is already perfect and take comfort and strength in that knowledge. Remember too that you can research other techniques and combine them if you wish or if you feel it is necessary! Search and experiment. Try each one in turn as various techniques are more effective than others for different people. You can then choose the ones you feel most comfortable with and maybe combine them for increased protection, if desired.

House Clearing

You can have your house cleared either by a Reiki Master, a psychic, a Catholic Priest or, alternatively, you can do it yourself. A Reiki Master will go from room to room using symbols to clear and seal out unwanted energy. Techniques vary. I always place the Cho Ku Rei on all four walls, the ceiling and the floor before drawing a final seal in the center of the room. If I have not done a clearing in a long time I will sometimes use a smudge stick to draw the symbols or smudge the room and then use the symbols in the manner I just described. Catholic priests normally say a prayer before a clearing and afterwards they bestow a blessing on the house and all who dwell within it. They will then go around the house, sprinkling all four corners and sometimes the center of each room with Holy Water. Closets should not be overlooked.

While finding a priest is a fairly easy task, finding a psychic or clairvoyant that you will feel comfortable with can be a different matter. There are many options for someone who is trying to locate a psychic for guidance or help. Shops that specialize in metaphysical books and crystals usually have staff that are aware of psychics in the area and they are usually very accommodating and willing to give guidance as to which psychic they would recommend and why. Alternative and complementary healers, such as Reiki Masters who are often psychic themselves, can be queried about clearing your house themselves. Venues where you can take classes on meditation and yoga are also a good place to inquire and get recommendations. There are also websites that list mediums and psychics that have trained with specific individuals or schools as well as Reiki Masters in your area. Even if the person you contact is not able to help with your specific situation, they should have a network of people that they can recommend. So just be brave and start asking questions!

Be sure to talk to any psychic or Reiki Master you choose first to discuss what your personal situation is and to express what it is you are looking for. Be open and don't be shy. It can feel awkward at first discussing things that you may have kept secret or that you have been made to feel stupid or uncomfortable about for many years. But remember, these individuals will not think you are crazy and they would have experienced much of the conflicting emotions and thoughts that you are housing within yourself. They will understand. In the end, when choosing what type of person to turn to for help or which specific individual to work with, go with your gut instinct – that is your own personal psychic intuition which should not be discounted. If you do not feel comfortable with someone, if you feel that you cannot establish trust with an individual, then find another one. It is better that you wait a little longer and find someone you trust than to rush into the care of someone you feel uncomfortable with. Take heart, you will find the right person to help you!

Smudge Sticks & Incense

Smudge Sticks are bundles of white sage that are a Native American tradition and are very effective in clearing rooms and balancing the energy of a place or person. You do not specifically need a Smudge Stick as a branch of dried sage will do just as well. To clear rooms, light the Smudge Stick and walk around the edge of the room (e.g. along each wall) waving the smoke toward the walls with hand movements. You can also wave the smoke around the center of the room.

To clear a person have them stand outside with their arms and legs spread out. Holding the Smudge Stick in one hand and using a waving motion with your other hand, direct the smoke around their bodies beginning from the top of the head, moving down one side of the body and going up the other, remembering to include the inner leg area. You are basically outlining the body first before repeating this action down the front and the back of the person. This clears the aura. As with any other ritual, this procedure will vary from person to person, so if someone suggests a different method that you find more appealing or effective then substitute it for the one I have outlined here. Remember, there is not only one right way of doing things.

Burning incense also clears space. If it is the first time you have cleared a room or have done any energy work in a room, then you can use it in the same way as the Smudge Stick. For long term, daily cleansing you can just light the incense and leave it burning. There is no need to manually circle it around the room.

Sound

Sound is also a very effective way to clear space. Some people use drums or bells, both of which are extremely effective. Drumming is great fun and is therapeutic as well. Unfortunately I have not yet taken classes, but I have friends who do African drumming or play the Bodhrán (the Irish drum) and their technique is to sit in the center of a room and play for as long as they want. They enjoy it, they get practice, and they clear the space all at once. I do not use bells because I find them too hard on my ears, but they are very effective. Bells can be used in the center of the room or you can walk around the room ringing them.

I use Tibetan cymbals, or Ting Sha, when I feel I need a little extra help clearing a space. Ting Sha are small cymbals that are attached to one another by a thin leather strap. I begin in one corner of a room and, holding the leather strap close to the cymbal, I strike them together on their edges, holding the one in my left hand still while gently whirling the one in my right, although sometimes I move both. As they resonate I raise them up towards the ceiling and then down towards the floor. I do this slowly and repeat as many times I as feel is necessary before taking a few steps sideways and repeating the process all over again. I make my way around the room, not forgetting the doorway. I also do the center of the room.

Salt Baths

Salt baths are another wonderful and very relaxing way to clear low or negative energy. Whether you use rock salt, table salt, Epsom salts, or salt with aromatic oils or herbs just be sure of two things – that the salt does not contain any artificial additives and that you soak in the bath for at least 15 minutes. If you don't have a bathtub then grab a bowl or bucket and soak your feet instead in the same manner. The toxins and low energy will be drawn through the feet.

Crystals

There are many books that deal with crystals and their properties, what they are used for, and how they can be employed effectively, so I won't go into this in any great detail. Clear quartz crystals are very good as an overall protective measure as they act as a sponge, absorbing negative energy. Because of this they should be cleansed regularly or the negative energy that has built up in them will begin to affect you. Some people recommend soaking them in salt water overnight, while others suggest submerging them under running water or placing them in sunlight for eight hours or so. Some bury them in the garden for several days to several months. Follow what feels best for you. When buying a crystal for a child, bring them with you and let them choose their own. They will always be drawn to the one that is best for them – the one they need at the time. Trust them. If they pick pink quartz instead of a clear one do not argue with them. They are being drawn to the pink crystal and must need the specific energy that this crystal can provide them with.

Please don't buy crystals just to have them. Remember that crystals are mined and are a result of us ripping into Mother Earth in order to access most of them. Now that crystals are so popular and human beings are so numerous, crystal mining is occurring on a huge scale and is a booming business. I am not suggesting that people should deny themselves the benefit of crystal "power", but please approach each purchase with consideration and respect for the huge amount of work and time that has gone into the Earth forming these crystals and the damage we are doing to her in order to remove them for our benefit. Also keep in mind that every crystal we take from Mother Earth denies her of their beneficial properties. If you have friends who have crystals, and there are crystals that you only require for a period of time, it may be worth considering forming an informal group where you can "sign out" and borrow or share crystals, although I do recognize that in many cases this may not be either feasible or convenient.

Meditation & Prayer

Finally, there can't be enough said about the power and benefits of meditation or prayer. Just be sure that whichever you choose, and it may be both, that you see, state, or intend your purpose with clarity and conviction. The Universe is ready and willing to help you in any way, but it needs to know with certainty what you need. It is also important to realize that there is sometimes a difference between what someone wants and what someone needs. We often confuse the two. We must keep in mind that things cannot come to us if we are not ready or if there are lessons we must learn before a request can be honored and fulfilled. It is also important to remember that we cannot interfere with the free will of others. So if your request interferes with the free will of someone else, it cannot be fulfilled. One thing to keep in mind, and one mistake that I often make, is that we can be presented with the answers to our prayers in a form that we overlook or do not recognize for what they are because they did not come in the packaging or manner that we expected. So praying for clarity of understanding and recognition is not a bad idea either!

Authors

I have read a good few books during my search for understanding and there are too many authors to list, but I thought I would list the names of a few who have contributed greatly to expanding my views, challenging my thinking, and provided me with information and understanding. Read these authors because they will expand your mind and your perceptions, and many answers will follow. Don't feel that you always have to agree with them, I know I didn't, and that is not the purpose of the exercise. We are all individuals and must come to our own answers in our own way. We are all here to learn and grow and the following people will certainly place you on that road. In alphabetical order these authors are: Carol Bowman, Gregg Braden, Dolores Cannon, Deepak Chopra, Steven Greer, Louise Hay, Caroline Myss, Eckhart Tolle, and Doreen Virtue.

A Final "Sign"

As I mentioned before, the Universe will provide you with answers, but sometimes you have to be paying attention. When I was about three-quarters through this book, doubt and fear reared their ugly heads. I began to question whether or not what I was sharing and writing would be of any use or interest to anyone. Was this a useless endeavor - a complete waste of time and effort? A floodgate of insecurity and doubt opened up and I stopped writing, finding any excuse not to sit down and finish this book. A few weeks into this I was at my favorite writing spot and lunch haunt, Flannery's in Glasheen, when Dawn, Laura, and Fiona (who basically run the place) asked me what I was writing. I had been going in there with my computer for months but they had never asked before. Sheepishly, I told them that I was writing a book and explained the subject matter to them. Their eyes lit up and the questions and interest began. Fiona, who has a little girl, began to share in a flood of words some of the "odd" things that she had experienced through her child. Her daughter had shared past life memories regarding an African family of which she was a part, who had a garden or were farmers. She inquired about her other mother and her other family, to which her current mother could not provide answers about. This child was also heard to hold conversations with a person that Fiona could neither see nor hear. When the child was asked who she was talking to, she would always reply, "To the man in the corner!" This story combined with their interest and excitement over what I was writing was exactly the motivation I needed to recommit myself to completing this book, and I am forever grateful to all of them for the discussion that day and their ensuing badgering for me to complete my book. I hope that they enjoy reading this as much as I enjoyed writing it.

Expect the Unexpected

"Expect the unexpected," seems like an obvious statement to make considering everything I have shared throughout this book, but I am still caught off guard by my children. Sometimes it is the content of their experiences and messages and sometimes it is the timing of when they choose to share. Other times such a long period has passed since the last event that I assume they have grown out of it or closed down their channels. I am always wrong!!

I had finished editing and was about to send off this manuscript when my daughter shared her latest experience with me. She had gotten up around six o'clock in the morning to go to the bathroom and then returned to bed. It was quite dark and she had just pulled the covers up over her shoulders when she noticed a large white ball of light hovering in the corner of the room. This ball was about 10 to 12 inches round but was only partially visible as a portion of it was hidden within the corner of the wall itself. This ball of white light was emitting a faint green light that was shaped somewhat like a crescent moon. This green light, that was about three feet in width, seemed to be growing in size in a pulsing, or paced, fashion and then shrinking back to its original size all at once. She watched it for some time before she noticed that the wall was moving slowly towards her. It continued until it was only a few inches from her face. It returned to its original position after she closed her eyes and wished for it to stop. She then noticed a light that was coming from behind her where there was a window. The light was pulsating and alternating with each pulse between a green light and a purple-blue light. This window is in another room and could not have been the source of the white ball with faint green light as the angle would not have allowed for that to occur. She found this a bit disconcerting as there is nothing behind that window but an acre-sized field that slowly rises into a hill and behind that is another massive field, not a road. This entire event lasted for over one hour although she said that it only felt as if a few minutes had passed.

I have no idea what this experience signifies or what the purpose or the source of it was, and if I take the time to analyze it yet another one will come my way and I will never complete this book! This experience shares aspects and traits of both spiritual and alien encounters. The white orb emitting green light is more spiritual; the wall moving could be either; and the pulsing lights though the window and the time distortion suggest alien involvement. So I will have to settle with merely sharing this amazing experience with you and hope that, at least for now, it will be enough. I assure you that any progress or updates in regards to this event will be posted on the Facebook page *A Knowing – Living with Psychic Energy* and on my website www.aknowing.com .

Where's the Beef?

There is strange and unusual activity and phenomena occurring all around us all the time. Just because all of us are not all capable of perceiving or experiencing them equally, or at all, does not negate their existence. The difficulty with this situation is that we have learned not to trust our inner-self or our innate psychic abilities as our society has developed over time into one that does not recognize things that are not measurable, quantifiable, or stamped with a seal of approval by a small group of individuals or institutions. Even when many individuals have experienced similar occurrences over extended periods of time in separate locations and societies, we still often require further confirmation from institutions that have put themselves forward as being authoritative in order for us to accept that something is true or real. When did we decide as individuals and as a race to hand over so much power to others? I can't answer that question but I can say that things are beginning to change. People are seeing and experiencing amazing phenomena and are no longer doubting these events or allowing institutions, authority figures, or other people to convince them that they are wrong or mistaken in their judgment of these experiences. We are taking back control. We are slowly deprogramming ourselves and learning to rely on our own instincts to decipher the events and activity that surrounds us and this is a wonderful thing. But for those who are still struggling, I have included two photographs that might help illustrate this unseen activity.

Cameras, especially digital ones, can capture what many of us cannot see with our naked eyes. The first picture, below, was taken by my mother with her digital camera. Everyone in the family looked at this picture, which I have cropped and enlarged to highlight the area of interest, and not one of us noticed anything strange. We **looked** but we did not **see**. My daughter Anithe explained this phenomenon when she told her father that you see with your mind not your eyes. We look around us and only take in what our minds have been programmed to acknowledge and let in. Therefore, we do not see much that exists because we have been trained to block it out. In this particular picture, that was taken in our living room, the camera somehow photographed the fruit bowl and the logo on the t-shirt that was behind my son's hands and arms. It is like an x-ray. His hands are not in motion and this cannot be a double exposure as it was a digital camera. The camera captured something that we have been taught is not possible based on our accepted understanding of how the world works. And yet part of my son is visibly invisible!

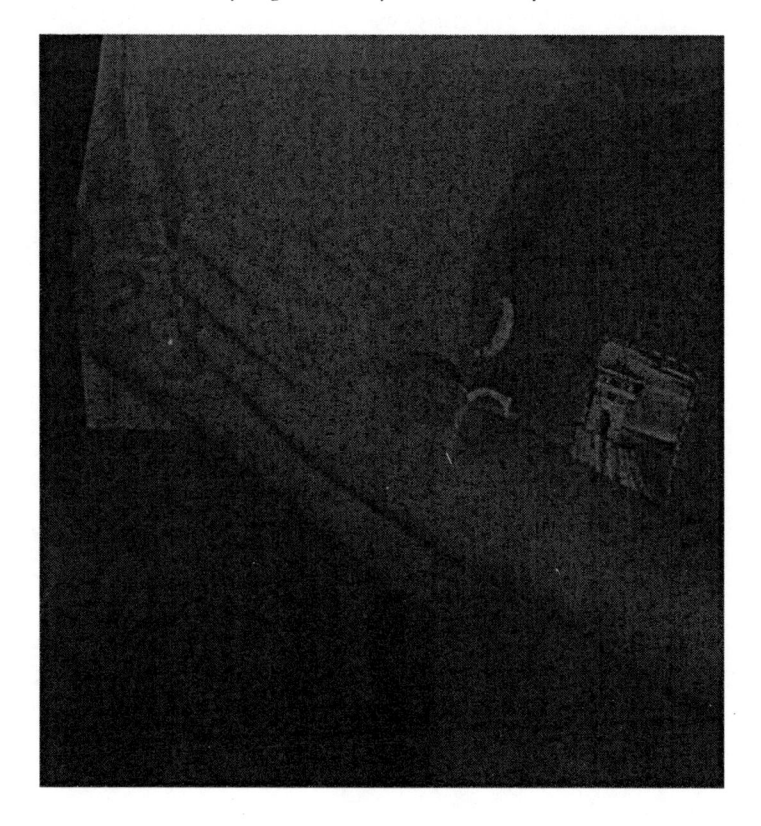

"X-Ray" Photograph

To see this in color go to www.aknowing.com or to the Facebook page: A Knowing-Living with Psychic Children

The second photo was taken by my best friend Siobhan with her digital camera and is of my daughter playing under our trees. Anithe appears to be engaging with multiple orbs of light, but I can assure you that none of us were aware of their presence at the time. The orbs are brilliant and of varying sizes, with some very small ones hovering just above the dirt on the left hand side of the picture. The children were playing and having a wonderful time and these entities were attracted to them, wishing to benefit from the positive energy that they were generating, which I think is wonderful. The more joy that can be spread and shared the better everyone will be – including those we cannot see.

Playing with Orbs

To see this in color go to www.aknowing.com or to the Facebook page: A Knowing-Living with Psychic Children

So things occur around us all of the time that we have been conditioned not to be aware of. These children come to us with an awareness, with untethered minds, and with many other tremendous abilities. All we have to do is find some way not to strip them of their abilities or cause them to shut down their gifts. We are in a time where we need these children and their gifts and energy more than ever. We need them to vibrate at their optimum level, perform their sometimes daunting tasks, and share their beautiful light. In the end, the choice is ours. What will we choose? I can only say that I hope we choose to support, honor, respect, trust and love these precious souls and allow them to shine their light into the darkness that we have created.

Afterwards

Speech given to UCC Psychological Society &

World Ghost Convention 2007

Good Evening. I was kindly invited to speak here tonight because I have had personal experience with the metaphysical and paranormal – much of it through my children. Children are really extraordinary and we tend to underestimate them. They are aware of much that we are not. Until the ages of approximately 7 to 9 they have not yet been fully conditioned to draw the veil between our world, our dimension, and the many others that intersect and interact with ours. So they see, feel, sense, and have knowledge of things that can and would amaze us…if we would only pay attention…if we would only take them seriously and not dismiss their valuable insights as being pure fantasy.

It is important for us, as adults, to relearn to open our minds to the many possibilities of "reality", for over time we have become boxed into a narrow definition of reality that **others** have constructed through fear, ignorance, or a desire to control. We relinquish great personal power when we accept the reality of others without question. The difficulty is that this process begins before we can start to question the origin, the motivations, the history, or the logic behind a belief system or a system of perception…we are indoctrinated from birth into the reality of our families and communities…and these beliefs become a way of life, a system we use to navigate life and make sense of the world we live in…they define the manner in which we perceive and decipher our environment.

When our personal reality is challenged, we tend to dig in and resist. This resistance can take many forms, the most common of which is to summarily discount other possibilities - other explanations, understandings and beliefs. It's difficult for us to alter our perceptions and our beliefs even when they are challenged by those we cherish, those we love, those we trust, those individuals who have absolutely nothing to gain by sharing their truths - our children. It's difficult because our belief system, our reality, is what we know, it's what we are comfortable with…it defines us and associates us with a group…it is the cornerstone from which we have launched ourselves into the world. It's also difficult because we fear being different, or being ridiculed or ostracized by our peers. Modifying or altering our sense of reality, our system of belief, is so challenging that we often ignore, discount, or explain away experiences that do not fit within our framework of what is possible…and this is what I would like to touch on tonight.

I feel that I was fortunate in that I was exposed throughout my life to two very different ways of thinking about the world. My mother, whose family came from the Middle East, leaned more towards a mystical view of life – a view that the thin veil is there, beings are all around us but most of us have lost the ability to see, sense and interact with anything beyond our three dimensional world. My father held a more traditional view – what you see is what you get, what the established institutions say is the closest you will ever get to the truth…anything else is either speculation or voodoo. My mother believed that when a baby smiled, in the way that they do, gazing off seemingly into nothingness, that they were smiling at angels for they were still so close to heaven they had not yet succumb to the blindness that afflicts the rest of us. My father believed that they had gas. Now, this was not his fault. This is what he was told by a figure of authority, a nurse in this case, on the day I was born.

The general attitude was, "babies are Tabula Rasa". They come into this world as clean slates, knowing nothing, able to contribute nothing, and the only reason they interact with the rest of us is either to satisfy their needs…or because they have gas. But are they Tabula Rasa? Certainly in terms of this life that we live here on Earth in this third dimension - in terms of rules, regulations, customs and beliefs - they are clean slates waiting to be written upon…imprinted, guided and taught. But I believe that they come to us with a great amount of insight and understanding, a deep knowing about the greater truths - the life beyond the veil - and these truths, this knowing, is often revealed in small observations and comments…in pure and precious statements which we often dismiss as fantastical or invalid. Now, I use the word **knowing** instead of knowledge, for that is what it is. Obviously young children have not accumulated knowledge through extensive research and study. However, they **know**, with every fiber of their being, that what they are saying and experiencing is true. It is something they just know without being able to explain how or why. So if we listen, if we open ourselves up to the precious information and knowing that children are able to share with us we would be amazed, we would be touched, and we would be comforted. It is their innocent understanding of existence before our Earthly incarnations, their acknowledgement of activity all around us, and their simple but wise insights that should confirm their knowing. In many ways, they should be teaching us.

When my children began to share their insights with me, I found myself torn between my mother's metaphysical and spiritual beliefs and my father's more practical and more widely accepted views. It was a struggle despite my having experienced many incidents throughout my life which pointed to the fact that there was more going on around me than I could register with my five senses. For example, there was an entity that regularly walked up and down the back stairs to my room and opened and closed my door…even leaving, again by opening and closing the door, when I asked him to. I say "him" because I believe that he was a young boy of about 7. But because I was never frightened by him, and because long periods passed between each visit, I never really thought much about it. There was the time when I was studying in a different part of our house waiting for my family to come home, when I heard heavy footsteps coming down the hall. Assuming that my father had returned and was coming to say hi, I looked up towards the closed door. The door swung open so violently it smashed off the wall…and no one was there. I held my breath and ran to the kitchen where I waited for everyone else to come home. I was afraid to go back to that part of the house on my own for several weeks, but when there was no repeat incident, and all returned to normal, I chose to ignore it. There was a bad smell in our living room that would begin fifteen minutes before guests would arrive and would disappear the minute the first person rang the bell. My mother solved the problem one night by entering the living room in a fury and threatening the entity with exorcism…we never had the problem again. I saw a boy of approximately 10 years old step off the end of our staircase…only the staircase had been remodeled and the return at the bottom from which he stepped had been removed…so I watched as he ran through the banister, through our dining room and into our living room. These are just a few examples of my own.

I would like to mention the point that skeptics often point to the fact that when individuals receive messages it can sometimes appear contradictory to information others have received, or they point to the imagery or source of the message being different as a way to prove that this phenomena, whether coming from children or adults, is not real. All information that comes from the Universe, comes through the filter that is the individual, and therefore the information is influenced by the person themselves. So a child from a Christian family will speak of Jesus and be given Christian symbols and references while a person from a different background will be given information that is in line with their religious beliefs or the beliefs of their community. It is important to keep this in mind and to remember that it is ***the deeper meaning of the message*** that is important, not the symbolic trappings that it comes in.

Before I go into some of the things that my children came out with, I would like to make it clear that my children are **not** unusual in this. More and more parents are reporting that their children are sharing extraordinary truths and insight into things that they should have no knowledge about. These insights come spontaneously, often leaving the parents speechless. At the time that my children began sharing things with me we were a family that did not attend church, nor did we discuss God or religion. My husband was Atheist and I was ambivalent at best. So you can imagine my surprise when, at age 4 ½ my son asked me, "Why do we have to die to go and be with God, when we were with Him already before?" or when he came running out of a room where he had been playing with his siblings to inform me that, "God Made Jesus. For God and Jesus, Life is Them. For Nature, God is Life," before running back out to rejoin the activity.

My children saw and described entities that I could not see, and colors or auras that surrounded others. They heard beautiful singing and saw clouds that emitted multicolored rain. They saw a bright blue light hovering at the foot of their beds and an angel with six wings. On reporting that they had been taught in school that people had only one chance to live my son age 6 ½ said, "Of course there's more than one chance…one chance would be silly. Some souls never come back to Earth…most do though. If a soul had a very hard time on Earth and suffered a lot, they might not want to come back, so they could choose to stay with God where there was love and they felt safe." A discussion between my kids that I overheard where one had expressed his fear of dying elicited this advice from his brother, "You **have** to die to go back to be with God **again**...and anyway, you don't have to worry because when you die you still live." At the age of 6 my daughter explained to me that "you see with your mind and not with your eyes". On the surface of it, this may not seem to be a remarkable statement, but she went into great detail in order to be sure I understood what she meant. An adult summary of her explanation is, "your beliefs define your perception". At 7 she shared the following insights, "There is no right way of saying God's name because God is everywhere, He is everything and He is everyone," and "God gave a piece of himself to everyone, but He is so great He can regenerate himself. There is God in all of us." To keep me on my toes in the early morning on our way to school my then 8 year old said, "I think the world is dimensions...See the dinosaurs are still here on Earth and you could see them if you could get into the right (time) dimension...It's all happening now at the same time."

But of all the forms of revelation that can come through children, my favorite type is the ones where I initially completely dismissed them as pure fantasy and wishful thinking, only to discover sometimes years later that there was much more to it. It is this type that keeps me humble and reminds me of how little I really know. In 2004, my 8 year old boy told me of how Jesus had visited him. Jesus had raised, or floated, him out of bed, surrounded him with **golden** and white light and proceeded to show him his inner qualities and beauty. I smiled, gave him an encouraging hug...wrote it down and thought – wishful thinking. I then forgot about it completely. You can imagine my surprise then, when two years later, as I studied the metaphysical and worked to become a Reiki Master, I discovered that the color of light attributed to Jesus – Christ light – is gold.

Considering the many unusual things I experienced in my life, I should not have been surprised or confused when my children began saying and experiencing things that are classed as out-of-the-ordinary... but I was. I was because, like most people, I had filed my experiences away in an attempt to disassociate from them and to undermine their importance and significance. I did this because society in general did not take people seriously who "believed" in a different reality or even in the possibility of a different reality. I did this because this is what I had been taught to do with things that were incongruent with the accepted norm, the seal-approved reality, and it was, therefore, what I felt most safe doing. Since that time I have become braver, and our society has become far more open and accepting, far more flexible with its definition of reality - but it still has a long way to go. Each and every one of us can contribute to this period of exploration and change, to this wonderful time of coming into knowing by being open to new ideas, and especially by listening to our children. Listen, learn and be amazed by these precious gifts that come to us in such small packages.

Now, I would like to share a few slides.